D1580906

RELATIONSHIP ANXIETY
DECLUTTERED

Simple Steps to Quickly Eliminate Anxious
Attachment, Insecurity, Negative Thoughts
and Conflicts in Your Relationship

INCLUDES THE 7-DAY SELF-LOVE CHALLENGE

JENNIFER HATHAWAY

Mango Broom Ltd

Email: sparkle@mangobroom.com

ISBN 978-1-913937-00-3 (eBook)

ISBN 978-1-913937-01-0 (print book)

First Edition

Legal and Disclaimer

YOUR FREE BONUS - 30-Days of Relationship Affirmations eBook!

As a way of thanking you for your purchase, I have a **free bonus** to offer you.

In addition to the information already provided in this book, I have created the *30-Days of Relationship Affirmations* eBook which provides you with 30 ready-made daily relationship affirmations. These will help you overcome any relationship roadblocks and strengthen your mind so that you can enjoy a more loving and intimate relationship.

Click (or tap) below to get your FREE Bonus instantly.

Click here:

www.mangobroom.com/relationship-affirmations/

CONTENTS

INTRODUCTION

ELATIONSHIP ANXIETY CAN lead to a life of misery and pain. It can leave sufferers unable to maintain romantic relationships, and it can turn marriage into a battleground. Dating becomes a horrific experience that usually results in people preferring to stay single and lonely. But it need not be like this. Many people find strategies to ease their anxieties and combat their fears, finally leading to fulfilling and happy lives.

This book speaks to people yearning to find happiness in a loving relationship. It recognizes the pain that men and women may go through in finding that special person they can rely on. Many readers will relate to the stories offered in each chapter. They help to unravel the complicated ways individuals internalize their emotions and their perceptions of who they are and what they contribute to the world in general.

Relationships can be the nicest thing on earth, especially loving relationships where both parties are friends and lovers. Sadly, they can also be ground zero for anxiety, and that can happen at any time in a relationship. Lots of single people quake at the thought of a relationship, instantly shrouded in stress and that can be caused by many things – maybe they have never been in a relationship before and are anxious about it, maybe they have seen their friends' relationships go down the drain because of anxiety and arguments, or maybe they were hurt badly in a previous relationship and its made them wary.

When you start dating someone, anxiety can kick in almost straightaway. Questions like, "Will this work?", "Is this a serious relationship?" or, "Do they really like me?" are bound to cross your mind. Sadly, in many cases, these worries never go away, even as a relationship kicks into higher gear and heads into the later stages. In fact, it's safe to say that as some couples draw closer, their anxiety levels rise. You can't stop thoughts, like "Is this really going to last?", "Is it going too fast?" or "I'm not sure I'm ready for commitment". These thoughts can flood through your mind, along with constant worry about whether your partner is still interested in you, or whether you are good enough for them.

When you get into a state of constant worry about a relationship, you can end up feeling quite lonely. No matter how close you think you and your partner are, constant anxiety creates a gap that just keeps getting wider, and, at its very worst, it can even result in you breaking up. The only way you can get out of constantly thinking and acting negatively (even subconsciously), is to identify that negative thought or action. Only then can you begin to deal with it.

When we fall in love with someone, it presents us with challenges we've never faced before. The more value you place in someone, the more you have to lose; on conscious and unconscious levels, we fear getting hurt. Everyone has a certain fear of intimacy, and that fear will often rear its ugly head just when things are going well for you, just when you think you've found the love of your life.

As you enter a relationship, lots of things can make you anxious, not just what goes on between the two of you. Your inner voice speaks up, criticizing you, giving you poor advice, telling you things like:

- "I'm too fat/uninteresting/not attractive enough to hold their interest."
- "Why bother? I'm never going to meet anyone decent, anyway."
- "I can't trust him/her; he/she is already on the lookout for someone else."
- "He/she doesn't love me. I need to get out before I get hurt."

It's this wicked inner voice – and we all have it – that makes us turn on ourselves and on those that we love. It can make you suspicious, paranoid, even hostile, and your self-esteem will plummet. It causes defensiveness, distrust, jealousy, and anxious feelings, feeding you a constant stream of negativity that makes you unhappy and worried, preventing you from enjoying what could be a fantastic relationship.

These negative and anxious thoughts are distractions that may stop you from relating to your partner properly. You might start showing destructive behavior, perhaps making snide comments or acting childishly. For example, your partner messages to say he must work late. You sit at home and as it gets later, your inner voice starts talking. It asks you, "Where is he?" "What's he really doing?" "He's never had to work late before; why now?" "Does he still love me?"

If you let your inner voice win, these thoughts will crash into one another, building up and, when your partner finally arrives home, you are almost completely paranoid, angry, insecure. You may be cold or irate towards him, and this causes your partner to go on the defensive, now frustrated and angry as well.

Soon enough, the dynamic that once existed between you has changed. Now, rather than enjoying yourself with him, the night has passed by in silence or in a blazing fight. That distance between you once feared is now there, *forced by you*. It isn't that he worked late that's caused this; it's your inner voice, distorting your thoughts and your perceptions, leading you on a path to destruction.

Throughout the pages of this book, readers will understand the cause of relationship anxiety, finding strategies and exercises to overcome relationship anxiety. They will learn to have a loving and contented relationship without being crippled by anxiety. This book is not intended for readers who may be struggling with violent relationships or who may have severe mental illness that requires the attention of a trained professional. You'll find no moral judgments about whether relationships are legal, civil, same-sex, or otherwise.

Now, be ready to delve into these pages for guidance, inspiration, and the constant reinforcing idea that you are unique and beautiful. Relationship anxieties can be conquered. This book will equip you with the knowledge of how to accomplish that, bringing you a loving and intimate relationship.

CHAPTER ONE
Understanding Relationship Anxiety

JENNIFER WAS NURSING *a failed relationship and desperately wanted to find someone who would love her unconditionally. For over five years, the man she had lived with had more than a controlling influence over her. So subtle was this control, she barely noticed it a first, but then, as time wore on, she realized that even an innocent chat with her partner would cause him to shut her down, turning the conversation around to him.*

There were no accusations of violent arguments; there was just this overbearing pressure on her to agree with everything he said or did. He always had an explanation ready when he didn't want to do things her way. This subtle bullying got to be too much, and she left the relationship.

Six months later, Jennifer met the man of her dreams. He was handsome, generous, and loving. They'd met at a mutual friend's wedding, and it was clear that David was a popular guy with both men and women. Gregarious by nature, he enjoyed sports and loved the company of others.

He loved Jennifer, too. All their friends agreed this was a partnership made in heaven.

For the past eight months, Jennifer and David had been living together, looking forward to getting married and raising a family together. There was little doubt they were the envy of their friends. But lurking beneath the surface of this happy relationship, Jennifer had such anxiety that her lover would change or find someone else that she was in danger of sabotaging the very thing she wanted most in the world: unconditional love.

She quizzed David if he was a little late coming home from work. She lay awake at night, going over and over earlier conversations looking for clues he was tired of her. She knew she was becoming needy and suffocating, but she couldn't stop. She loved him so much, but did he love her?

Because Jennifer's previous relationship had left her feeling demoralized and worthless, she found it hard to accept that someone else could find her worthy of loving.

Using authoritative sources and anecdotal stories, the following chapter will outline what relationship anxiety is and its possible causes, leaving you with some key takeaways to improve your relationships.

What is Relationship Anxiety?

New relationships can begin with a bang, or start with a whisper, promising happier times ahead. It doesn't matter if it's love at first sight or you grow into love, when you meet the love of your life for the first time, the moment is engraved in your memory forever. It keeps you awake at night and distracted by day. As love deepens, you begin to make plans. You learn to know each other's ways and grow to trust each other. For some, though, anxiety takes over; if you are reading this book, you may be one of these people.

You over-think everyday conversations with your partner. *What did he mean when he said your girlfriend seemed nice? Is he attracted to her? Should I be worried?* Then you casually flip through his texts when he leaves his phone on the kitchen counter. He frowns when you ask him for the third time where he went to lunch that day.

This is classic relationship anxiety, and it's more common than you might think. So why do some people constantly question their relationships? Why do some people push this anxiety to a point where the relationship simply breaks down?

Is My Behavior Normal?

Psychologists believe that relationship anxiety, particularly in the early stages of romance, is a normal reaction to the fear of the unknown. *Will he like me? Do I really like him?* However, it should be clarified that, at times, anxiety is a normal caring reaction, i.e., anxiety you may feel about your children, your parents, and others that you love when things are not going well for them is normal.

9

Relationship anxiety is the kind that goes too far, living inside your head, where you allow it to flourish and grow unchecked until it eventually manifests physically in emotional distress. This results in ill health, both physical and mental. Loss of appetite is a common symptom of anxiety, resulting in abnormal weight loss and stomach problems. Then along comes the feelings of exhaustion followed by loss of motivation.

In other words, you feel sick most of the time. You could say that the relationship is becoming toxic and is easily contracted by your partner. So, while a certain level of anxiety is normal in a loving relationship, when it gets out of hand, then "normal" becomes "abnormal," and the relationship sours.

How Do I Recognize if I Have High Anxiety in My Relationship?

When you allow room in your head for high levels of anxiety, there is an awful lot of chatter. It's like living with a noisy neighbor; there never seems to be any quiet. Your noisy neighbor is constantly asking you around, asking questions about your relationship, and bombarding you with negative suggestions.

He confuses you so much you find doubts are constantly crowding your head; those doubts lead you to try to find answers to questions about a future that may or may not happen. If all this sounds very chaotic, *it is*. Relationship anxiety can be a very real and worrisome experience, and recognizing the symptoms is a good place to begin your journey of recovery. Consider the questions below. Are you sitting in your head?

Does He Really Care for Me?

It is normal to ask yourself if your partner cares for you. If your relationship is new, then you shouldn't be investing in it long term if you suspect he doesn't care for you as much as he should. This is a fundamental question you should ask yourself when a new relationship begins.

Relationship anxiety becomes worrisome when you are constantly asking yourself this question. It gets worse still when you are constantly asking your partner, which you know, deep down, is futile because if he hasn't gone already, the answer will be yes.

So instead, you internalize the question. *Does he miss me when I'm not there? Why isn't he always willing to support me when I need him? Is he happy just so long as we are having sex?*

Often there is very telling evidence these questions loom too large in your head. For instance, how often in a day do you text your partner on the most trivial matters? How much time do you spend waiting for his reply? Why is he not responding immediately? Doesn't he care?

When he does reply, how long do you stare at the text trying to read things into the reply that are not there? Remember that we all do this when we meet someone we are deeply attracted to; it's part of the romance, part of the chemistry. However, when you

11

become obsessed with looking at your cellphone, you are becoming obsessed with those doubts in your head, and this is not good for you or your relationship.

Am I a Saboteur?

Many of us who have experienced the pain of breaking up find it hard to accept that it might have been *us* who have caused a relationship to fall into tatters. But let's be reflective here. How often have you picked a fight with your partner just to test the strength of the relationship?

This sounds a little whacky, but psychologists agree that subconscious sabotage is quite common for people who feel insecure. Believing that their partner is about to end the relationship, or that they don't care enough, they create situations in which their partner has to prove that they care.

Another way this sabotage is played out is doing things without telling your partner, like meeting an old boyfriend for a coffee and only telling your partner *after* the event. Turning to friends or family members instead of your partner, in times of need, is also a sabotaging strategy. Both approaches are usually done subconsciously.

The problem with these tactics is that your partner is not likely to pick up on what you are doing – subconsciously or not – leaving them confused and upset. Therefore, the likelihood of your partner enacting the fears living inside your head becomes real.

Is He Going to Break Up with Me?

A healthy, loving relationship is nurtured by trust and feelings of security. Most of us agree this is what we strive for and would do anything to keep things that way; naturally, we want to nurture our relationship and do the best we can to keep the relationship strong.

However, if the task of keeping your relationship intact is making you feel ill, then it is affecting your well-being and needs to be addressed. Staying overly-concerned about keeping a relationship together is a symptom of relationship anxiety that can have worrisome outcomes.

For example, do you submit to your partner's requests to keep him happy? *Yes, we'll go eat sushi*, even though you both know you hate sushi. That might sound trivial, but what if your partner frequently arrives home late, giving no explanation? Do you keep quiet rather than cause an argument? Changing your behavior to suit another person is never a good idea.

Relationship anxiety does have some very negative impacts on health and well-being, but the unease of trying to keep the bond intact is probably one of the most negative aspects. There is a genuine need to openly discuss the boundaries and behaviors you expect from your partner – accepting the consequences, good or bad. This is a brave thing to do when we desperately want to hold onto the man we love but adjusting our behavior to fit someone else's *bad* behavior is never good.

Showing jealousy is also destructive. It may stem

from your fear of losing your partner, but it is counter-productive and will probably lead to the breakdown of the relationship or, at the very least, an unhappy existence for both partners. Consider the story below:

"I always worried that Lloyd would leave me for someone else. He was so handsome, and I often caught women taking a second glance at him when we were out together. I felt a strong need to watch his every move. I wanted to know where he was all the time.

When he came home at night, I questioned him about whether he had spoken with any women that day. He always said no, but I knew that was a lie, so I would continue to badger him until he gave me an answer I wanted to hear. Yes, he had spoken to his colleague, Janice, over the phone for a few minutes about work. So, then I would question him about Janice. Did he find her attractive? Did she flirt with him? That kind of scenario would play out every evening in our home until one day, Lloyd just left.

He gave no reason. He just packed his bags and left, thus, proving I was right to be anxious about our relationship." (Miranda, age 26)

There are many tell-tale signs in relationship anxiety. Over-thinking things, worrying about whether your partner loves you as much you think they should, wondering why they don't do enough to show their love and affection, constantly questioning their motives. If these thoughts fill your head with noisy chatter that keeps you awake at night and causes you endless stomach-churning anxieties, then you have relationship anxiety, and now's the time to ask yourself *why*.

You must know the difference between normal anxieties that are a natural response when we love someone, and relationship anxiety so obsessive that relationships fail.

Possible Causes of Relationship Anxiety

It is one thing to recognize the symptoms of relationship anxiety and quite another to admit that behind these symptoms may lie serious personal issues you need to deal with. We are quick to recognize faults in others, but a bit slower to admit faults in ourselves.

This book will help you to reflect on some issues that have caused you pain in your relationships, and it will also provide some tools to help dig your way out of the anxiety that has hindered your love life. When things are too overwhelming to cope with on your own, seeking help from a professional therapist is the best way forward. This book is not intended to replace professional help.

However, if you are prepared to look inwards and will face some of your inner demons, you are more likely to develop a better understanding of what triggers your anxiety. That way, you become better able to deal with it – if not abolish it entirely. So, let us consider some causes of relationship anxiety.

I Always Bring My Previous Relationship Experiences into My Next One

This is a "biggy" when it comes to new relationships as, often, previous ones have ended on a sour note. Even if we leave a romantic partnership on good terms, we should make a mental list of all the things we didn't like about it in an effort not to make the same mistakes again.

For instance, how often have you thought: *"I always wanted my ex to be more sporty instead of sitting watching TV all of the time."* Or, *"I hated that my ex was so stingy with his money"*. Next time, subconsciously or not, you'll look for a mate that does not display these traits.

Even if you do end up with a "sporty" guy who is not stingy with his money, negative experiences with an ex can still have a profound impact on the way you view your next relationship. The subsequent result can be extreme relationship anxiety.

"We were married for seven years before we decided to call it a day. We'd met in high school, and we married after graduation. We had no children, and I think we got together too young, so when we split it was by mutual agreement. When I met Chris, I was immediately smitten. He was so generous with his money. Jake, my ex, had always been careful with money. True, we hadn't got much because we married young, but his meanness with money caused me a great deal of anxiety. Chris was like a ray of sunshine in my dreary life.

Expensive restaurants and unexpected bouquets of flowers turned my head, and before long, we were engaged to be married. Only then did I discover that, unlike Jake, who had taken his family responsibilities very seriously, Chris had a cavalier attitude towards money and told me he couldn't contribute to the cost of the wedding because he was deeply in debt. I realized that if I went ahead with the marriage, I would, yet again, spend my entire life worrying about money." (Charlotte, age 29)

Betrayal

What if your ex cheated on you? Have you brought this experience into your current relationship? Is this why you have sleepless nights and constantly go through your partner's pockets when he gets home, even though you know it's wrong?

Experiencing betrayal is a hard knock to take in life and, unfortunately, we often carry it with us into the next relationship. Placing trust in another can be difficult; no one wants to get hurt a second time. When we experience certain vulnerable behaviors, even words said casually can trigger memories, making us feel insecure in our relationships.

When we feel insecure, our anxiousness impacts our relationship, however secure it may be in reality.

Being too Needy

No one likes to think they are needy, so this trait needs real reflection. If you suspect you are too needy, you need to ask yourself why. Psychologists posit that being needy stems from childhood experiences of attachment. Consider what the renowned psychologist, John Bowlby, says about attachment. *"…attachment behaviors are instinctive responses to the perceived threat of losing the survival advantages that accompany being cared for and attended to by the primary caregiver(s)"* *(Ackerman, 2020. P.1).*

To put this in another way, if your needs were met promptly when you were a child, then you probably grew up with well-developed attachment traits. When needs are not met as a child, we become less secure.

While accepting this may seem difficult, ask yourself if your anxiety about commitment is because you are afraid your needs may not be met. When you do commit, are you constantly afraid that your partner will suddenly disappear from your life? When discussing theories of this sort, nothing is written in stone. Yes, some of us may have attachment issues that go a long way back.

This doesn't mean we *must* be needy or constantly live in fear that our loved ones will leave us. Life experiences can change us, and we can learn to grow. When we adjust to these fundamental character traits, we can become more secure.

Low Self-Esteem

If you are transitioning from a failed relationship into a new relationship, it is not uncommon to have low self-esteem. It's often difficult to get back up after having had our confidence knocked, but how well you survive this knock-back depends on your inner strength and your willingness to accept the love of a new partner.

If you feel you are unworthy, you may have grave doubts about what your new partner thinks about you. Does she think you are unworthy too? Of course she doesn't; she's in a relationship with you! Yet, you may be thinking, "She doesn't know me yet, wait until she finds out what I'm really like."

In this case, you are projecting your own thoughts onto someone else, leading to problems in your relationship. The antidote to this is to work on your low self-esteem.

KEY TAKEAWAYS

- Anxiety is a normal response when we feel threatened, and normal when related to the well-being of those we love.

- Relationship anxiety becomes problematic when it causes emotional distress, jealousy, and self-doubt. When this type of anxiety sets in, we begin to over-think innocent remarks and conversations made by our partners. We begin to suspect them of not being loyal, or we imagine they are cheating behind our backs. In the end, we may sabotage the relationship in our quest to protect ourselves.

- Relationship anxiety is generally the result of a variety or a combination of experiences and emotions. We may have feelings of insecurity, so we are overly needy in our relationships. We may subconsciously bring our past experiences in our new relationships, believing that what went wrong previously is bound to happen again in the current relationship.

- Many of us have feelings of low self-esteem when entering a new relationship, because we believe we have failed in some way or because a previous partner worked hard to convince you that you were unworthy. If the latter is the case, then it may be time to throw caution to the wind and leave the past where it belongs; live for the here and now because the future has not been written yet.

The signs of relationship anxiety are not exhaustive; they come in many guises. How can we know for sure that our own anxieties are contributing to our relationship difficulties?

The following chapter provides detailed clues into how to recognize you may have relationship anxiety.

CHAPTER TWO

How Do You Know If You Are Suffering From Relationship Anxiety?

"To BE HONEST, *I'd never really been in a serious relationship before. I'd had lots of boyfriends and quite a few 'friends with benefits.' Not that that I have loose morals or anything like that, it was just that I was single. I had a good job, and I was enjoying my life. Then Greg walked into my life, and I felt like I'd been hit with a sledge-hammer. We were introduced at a party, and as soon as we shook hands, I knew this was the guy I'd been looking for all my life. We started dating, and I couldn't have been happier.*

I was anxious about the relationship from the start. I'd never really been head-over-heels in love before, so I thought I was just 'love-sick,' and if this was what being in love was like, I'd just live with my anxieties, in fact, I exhausted myself trying to please him. The more I tried to please him, the more distant Greg seems to become. He didn't complain, but he didn't thank me either. Then one day, my sister made me realize that I had become obsessed with trying to please my partner, and it was not only ruining my health, it was also ruining my relationship." (Carole, age 34)

As the above testimony shows, no one teaches us how to behave when we fall in love. Some of us fall in love with the idea of love without knowing what it is; some of us are so smitten by this new person in our lives and don't notice our anxiety levels rising. This chapter discusses how you can tell if you are experiencing a normal reaction to being in love or whether your anxiety is damaging your relationship.

Common Signs You May Have Relationship Anxiety

You Have Become Possessive and Jealous

You constantly question your partner's whereabouts. *Why are you going out? My friend Sarah saw you talking to a woman today. Who is she? What's her name? Have you met with her before?* The thought that your partner is speaking to someone of the opposite sex causes you so much anxiety, you begin laying down rules you expect your partner to follow. *I want you home straight after work. I don't want you to go out with your friends anymore. I want you to stop going to the Gym.*

The more your partner complies with your possessiveness, the more possessive you become. You go out for dinner, but you insist that you choose where you sit in the restaurant. You make sure there are no attractive women near your table. You watch him closely when he goes to the bar for drinks.

If you think you are alone dealing with this destructive trait, you are wrong. Even celebrities can be subject to the green-eyed monster. A few years back, Beyoncé became jealous of her husband, Jay-Z's, friendship with Rihanna, which resulted in a public fit of jealous rage being played out in a restaurant.

Psychologist David Buss suggests that jealousy in a relationship can be a real threat. In its extreme form, jealous partners will constantly try to belittle their partner to convince them they could never find anyone else to love them (Eckel, 2016).

Are You too Attached to Your Partner?

Listen to any love song, and you will hear words of undying love. "…go to the ends of the earth for you," Adele sang. Not surprisingly, many of us become hopelessly devoted to the new passion in our lives; still, becoming *too attached* can spell danger for a relationship.

If you think you are too attached, ask yourself: how many times have you texted your lover today? What was his reaction when you gave him a keyring with your name engraved on it? Or God forbid, showed him your latest tattoo with his name stenciled onto an unmentionable part of your anatomy?

According to a study conducted at the University

25

of Hong Kong in 2012, people with attachment issues do one of two things: require or demand an intimate relationship too soon, or run away from romances in which the partner requires a closer relationship too soon. (Whitborne, 2012)

Either way, the culprit is the fear of being abandoned. Yes, adult love hurts, but there is always another love waiting around the corner, so, take it nice and easy.

Do You Punish Yourself Unmercifully When Things Go Wrong?

So far, we've discussed how relationship anxiety can make us behave in ways we would probably frown upon when done by others. Still, relationships can be tricky, especially new relationships.

Some end after the first night of passionate sex. The proverbial "one-night-stand" may not have started out as such, but somewhere in those passionate fun-filled hours, something goes wrong, and by morning, you are left feeling used and ashamed. Don't do this. Remember that you are a consenting adult.

So many people, and it is generally women, beat themselves up unmercifully when they do something they regret. If you had fun, let it go. If you hurt another person with thoughtless actions or words (often, we don't know how to extricate ourselves from an awkward situation, so we just get up and leave), just apologize, forgive yourself, and move on. Blaming yourself when relationships don't work can lead to problems in a new relationship because you bring shame with you unnecessarily.

Are You a Self-Silencer?

We are taught from an early age to hold our tongue; if you can't say something nice, then say nothing. But the problem with self-silencing in a relationship is that it can make you ill.

A recent study from Pittsburgh University found that women who held their tongue to keep the peace in their relationships were more likely to damage their heart health than women who expressed their feelings openly (Bronner, 2020).

This is serious stuff. What are you doing when you adopt a self-silencing approach in your relationship? Well, you are *sitting inside your head*.

Health experts believe that you are attempting to contaminate your relationship. You fear that if you express your feelings and emotions, your partner will disapprove, and he will leave you. This can be a somewhat learned characteristic, as many people are taught not to show their emotions, making them seem cold and aloof; the thoughts inside of your head may tell a different story.

All the unsaid words and feelings are being played out secretly, and this is relationship anxiety at its worst. Stress and anxiety are often caused by our inability to express our thoughts and feelings. We see this in the workplace with people holding their tongue for fear of losing their jobs.

Unfortunately, it also happens in relationships too. If you are a self-silencer, it's time to unleash that beast sitting in your head, not just for the sake of your relationship, but for your health too.

Do You Over-Analyze Everything?

Over-analyzing every little thing your partner does and says is exhausting; it's also addictive. If you over-think things, you know how this feels; a chance word or action from your partner leads you into creating scenarios that have not happened – and probably never will. You believe that your overanalyzing is a good thing. *I am prepared*, you tell yourself. *It's just the way I am made.*

But these stories you create in your head are based on your imagination, not real events. Take Susan, for example:

"He said he'd been asked to attend a conference in Ohio and that he'd be away for three days. He'd been away from home on business before, so at first, I thought nothing of it. But I noticed that he'd bought new clothes for the trip and he seemed overly excited about the conference. After all, it was just for work, right? I looked at the conference up on the internet, and then I found I couldn't stop. I began searching for bars and restaurants. I even 'googled' the nightclubs, even though I knew he was never into the nightlife. I questioned him about what his room was like and what his plans were when the day's work was finished. I inquired

from some colleagues whether they were going, too. In the end, I was convinced that my husband was seeing another woman. I could even see her in my mind's eye, what her hair color was, what clothes she wore. When I imagined her in bed with my husband, I just lost it. I told him he couldn't go and would have to call in sick. He was so taken aback by my meltdown he <u>did</u> call in sick. Things never really recovered after that, and our marriage just started to crumble away." (Susan, age 35)

If this is you, then it's time to take stock. Why do you think you are doing this? Look inside yourself rather than looking into a future that's not even here.

Are You Waiting for Your Partner to Fix Your Anxiety?

If you suffer from relationship anxiety, it can make you extremely selfish. Often, over-anxious individuals look to their partners to ease their worries. Like Susan in the story above, insisting that your partner desists from activities to ease your anxiety is a recipe for disaster.

How often do you get all riled up about going to dinner with your partner's business colleagues because you don't feel confident?

These events cause you anxiety – and expecting your partner to fix this is unrealistic, and it is selfish. Often, mothers get anxious about leaving children with babysitters and expect their husbands to call to make sure the kids are okay, which distracts from the intimate, special time the couple has together.

Your fears and your concerns can be eased to a degree with the help of supportive partners but if you put unnecessary pressure the relationship, things will get stressful, and your partner may become unresponsive to your needs. Your partner cannot always fix your anxieties; if you're expecting it, you may be waiting a long time.

Are You Afraid of Making a Long-Term Commitment?

Many singles admit to avoiding commitment to a relationship. Five years ago, when Actress Michelle Rodriquez carved a glittering career for herself, she admitted that she found it hard to make a long-term commitment, saying that the longest she ever stayed in a relationship was six months. (Your Tango, 2020)

This is more common than you may think, and this resistance can lead to relationship anxiety from the onset of a new romance. Making a long-term commitment is a serious step, usually taken when couples have been dating for some time and wish to take the relationship to the next level.

However, for some individuals, that next step may be a step too far. Individuals with commitment issues will begin a process of withdrawal almost from the beginning. This can be seen shortly after the relationship begins or some weeks later.

A lot of psychological research surround the issue

of commitment. As discussed briefly in the previous chapter, according to psychologists, attachment in early life impacts adult life significantly; this is often seen in adults whose parents/caregivers were unresponsive to their needs or who were overly demanding.

These adults tend to be very independent and self-reliant, having learned at an early age that adults can be unreliable. This is carried through into their adult romantic relationships. If you are among those individuals who find it difficult to commit to a long-term relationship for fear that your partner will let you down, it's time to do a little soul-searching and have a little faith. We don't always get it right, but at least we can try.

Do You Turn Small Problems Into Big Ones?

"My boyfriend throws his dirty socks on the floor when he gets into bed," says Victoria, a legal recruiter in New York. "Once a man is living with a woman, he doesn't really see the need to clean up after himself. He assumes I'll just pick them up in the morning. It's disrespectful." (Dixit, 2020)

We all recognize this type of irritant. Is it a big issue or a small one? Well, it all depends on your level of relationship anxiety. Of course, people should clean up after themselves unless they are a small child.

Relationship break-ups are peppered with stories about partners' small irritating habits that, in the end, get the better of us. Here are a few complaints men and

31

women make about their partners. Where do you stand on some of these: guilty or not guilty?

According to Psychology Today (2009), a common complaint that men have about women is that they are experts at giving the "silent treatment." Women are also adept at reviving things that happened in the past and making them part of a current argument. Men also say that women are too critical about how men do things around the house.

Women's complaints about men include that they forget significant events such as anniversaries and birthdays. Many women also find personal habits such as breaking wind or burping in public irritating.

Eying up women is a real irritant that can blow up into a big issue if not handled well. Small irritants can become big issues that create real fissures in a relationship. According to some experts, "You don't really live with the partner at home. You live with your partner in your head." (Dixit, 2020, p.1.)

In other words, as your connection blossoms and irritants become more irritating, you believe that your partner is self-centered, and so start building up evidence you can use against them. If yours has reached this level of anxiety, it's time to discuss it with your partner; beware, he could find this extremely irritating!

Do You Want to Control Everything?

We all want things to run smoothly. How often have you said to yourself, "I'll just take care of this because it's easier, and I know it will get done"?

The problem with this attitude is that it becomes a way of life, and either you will eventually be put upon and thus resent having to do everything yourself, or the people around you will tire of your controlling behavior. Consider this story from Psychology Today (2010):

"My mind quickly races through a list of people I love or care about, or maybe even just met or heard about, reviewing in my mind the pressing issues, needs, and problems of anyone or anything that may need my attention or my help that day. Next, my mind turns to the list of things that my husband or my two children need to do. I have to be sure that no one forgets anything that might cause problems later. If I don't come up with anything significant, I might search further into what might happen in the future that could be prevented if only I could think of it and take some action. I am exhausted before I start."

This woman is obviously a caring person and wants to do what she considers best for her family and friends. What she is unaware of is the intrusive nature of her controlling ways that imply that without her interference, the family would fall apart.

Her belief she can control not only her own destiny, but that of her family and friends, is making her ill. Relationships can be put under enormous pressure when one partner tries to take away the autonomy of the other.

If this is you, try to recognize that this is relationship

anxiety. You want everything in your life to be right, and you believe that by taking control, you are pre-empting disaster. It's time to start exploring relationship anxiety and asking yourself if controlling your partner is storing up problems for the future.

Do You Lack the Confidence to Determine the Course of Your Relationship?

Deep within ourselves, we know when we are suffering from low self-esteem, even if we don't admit it out loud. Inside of a relationship, your low self-esteem can worsen. Consider some signs that may indicate you have low self-esteem.

How often do you ask permission to do even the simplest of things? Before you consider this, we are not talking about being polite and caring towards those around you. If you ask permission to do everyday things such as leaving the room or visiting a friend – or even asking permission to change the channel on the TV – then it could be that you have low self-esteem. You are attempting to validate your behavior.

You are looking for approval from your partner, which can cause significant anxiety in a relationship for both partners. You may be indicating to the world and your partner that you don't want to cause a fuss; you don't wish to interrupt the lives of those around you, and you certainly don't want to inconvenience him/her.

Another sign you're suffering from low self-esteem is that you hardly ever tell the truth about how you feel – what you secretly think about your life, your relationship, or your personal experiences. Some individuals embellish their life history to make themselves appear more confident: a sure sign that relationship anxiety is controlling your life.

KEY TAKEAWAYS

- Possessiveness and jealousy are powerful emotions that lead to high levels of relationship anxiety for both partners.

- Becoming too attached to a partner indicates you may have attachment issues. Needy partners invariably end up in broken relationships or being controlled by a dominating partner.

- Punishing yourself over past indiscretions (both perceived and real) leads to low self-esteem and is easily transported with you into a new relationship.

- Self-silencing is commonly attached to relationship anxiety, and evidence suggests that it also contributes to serious health issues.

- At time, most individuals over-think. Over-analyzing everything that your partner does or says is detrimental to a happy and contented relationship.

- Your partner cannot fix your relationship anxiety. It is not their job to do that.

- Having issues with long-term commitments may be better solved by consulting a therapist. Long-standing attachment issues are hard to come to terms with on your own.

- Don't turn the little irritations into big ones. Deal with them openly and with honesty.

- Do not try to control those around you.

Individuals with controlling partners are more likely to become unresponsive and apathetic.

• Low self-esteem is crippling in a relationship. Therapy is an effective way to overcome low self-esteem.

Recognizing the signs you may have relationship anxiety is an important start in improving your relationships, but how about your partner? What do you do if your partner has relationship anxiety? The following chapter offers discussion about the most common signs that your partner is suffering from this debilitating kind of issue.

CHAPTER THREE

Signs That Your Partner May be Suffering from Relationship Anxiety

"IT WAS THE day before we were due to fly to Iceland that I noticed Mike seemed quiet and anxious. I began to feel anxious too! I knew that Mike was impulsive when he got anxious and would change his plans at the drop of a hat, giving some kind of wild excuse. We'd been planning this trip for a year. Surely, he couldn't be having second thoughts, not the day before our departure. I kept up a steady chatter throughout the day, trying to judge his mood. I asked him outright at one point, 'Are you looking forward to our adventure?' He nodded, and I felt obliged to not ask again. The next day arrived cold and crisp. It was February in New York, and snow lay on the ground. I busied myself with the final packing when Mike said with finality. 'I'm not going to Iceland. You will have to go alone.' I was expecting some sort of anxiety today – but not this. 'You can't do this to me,' I said. 'This vacation has cost us a fortune, and we won't be able to get our money back.'

'I'm not going,' he said bluntly. 'I had this dream that the plane crashes. I think it is an omen.' And that was that. Neither of us took the trip. I didn't want to go alone. But I realized, then, there was something wrong with our relationship. This anxiety was more than just a fear of flying; it hit at the very root of our marriage. I was living his anxieties instead of enjoying the good fortune that we'd accumulated over our six years of marriage." (Jennie, age 31)

Mike's behavior is not uncommon. Relationship anxiety manifests in many forms. Mike was using his fear of flying as a way to include Jennie in his bouts of anxiety. Could he have been blaming her for his own shortcomings? Below are seven signs that your partner may be suffering from relationship anxiety.

Is Your Partner Jealous and Possessive?

When the green-eyed monster comes to call on your relationship, it is a sure sign that something is wrong. If your partner is possessive or jealous of you, then this is something you must tackle, as jealousy can be very destructive.

The problem with a possessive partner is that when you first meet, that possessiveness is very alluring. Many people may be swayed by grand shows of affection and endearment. This may take the form of wanting to be around you all the time, wanting to share your activities – and even friendships. Being possessive is generally a characteristic born out of insecurity.

People who have grown up with overly protective parents can become jealous by nature when they become adults. Studies have shown that having overly-vigilant parents makes children less independent and clingy. (Eckel, 2016)

When a partner shows signs of affection or genuine interest in other people, the possessive partner may become very distressed and demand that contact with people outside of their immediate circle be cut. Perhaps Mike, in the story above, is jealous of the excitement and distraction that Jennie feels about the vacation. Jennie's attention is on this and not on her husband. Mike can easily sabotage the trip because he has done this his entire life to gain attention.

Is Your Partner an Avoidant?

Distancing strategies are often used by partners experiencing relationship anxiety. They avoid intimate relationships. They will start out as attentive romantic partners, but the signs are there early if you look carefully. You may be fooled, for example, by a partner who appears chivalrous but who avoids making sexual advances too soon after meeting.

They may avoid kissing too, maintaining they want the relationship to blossom as friendship to begin with. An avoidant will resist sharing a bed and may even back off when you get too affectionate. This is usually followed by a reluctance to voice endearment.

An avoidant partner will rarely say those magic words, "I love you."

This is because the next step may be a request from you for commitment. This is when you are likely to hear the words "I don't want to make a commitment at this stage." Avoidant partners can be very unsupportive and become disinterested in what you are doing.

Soon, the loud-and-clear message you hear is that of indifference to your everyday activities. They have removed themselves emotionally. They are more important than you are. This pattern of behavior will follow the avoidant throughout their lives unless they seek professional therapy. Having commitment issues stems from past experiences in childhood – experiences that could include poor parenting, or broken trust.

Is Your Partner Too Clingy?

Being clingy is usually associated with low self-esteem. Clingy individuals are attention seekers. Your partner may be too attached because they fear you will leave them. This is not a difficult trait to recognize, and often we recognize this in a partner, mistaking if for just a "personality thing." It can be romantic at the beginning of a relationship but can become exhausting as the relationship progresses.

Being too clingy can result from a past relationship that went wrong, perhaps leaving them with a broken heart. If your partner makes you exhausted with constant attachment to you, then perhaps it is worth delving a little deeper into his past relationships.

If he fears you will leave him, maybe you are having relationship issues as well, and his anxiety is feeding off *your* anxiety. However, a partner who demands constant attention and reassurance can be wearying – not conducive to a healthy, blooming relationship.

Does Your Partner Display Passive-Aggressive Behavior?

An easy way to assess whether your partner is passive-aggressive is to think about when you last tried to have a reasonable conversation in which issues got settled. Do they shrug and comply, but their body language says something different?

Think about the story that opened this chapter. Mike complied with the holiday right up to the day they were due to fly out. Then he sabotaged it. When we view the behaviors mentioned above, we could say that at some time, we've all indulged in these activities; being jealous, being needy, and sabotaging something before it fails us in some way. However, what we're talking about here is a pattern of behavior you *come to expect*. How often does your partner blame other people for things that go wrong in his life? How often does he lie to get out of a tight place?

Passive-aggressive individuals never like to stand up and be counted or be called to account. Living with a passive-aggressive partner can be tedious and exhausting; they'll never negotiate, no matter how important the issues. They will simply walk away, or they will accuse you of making things difficult. You will often discover that they make a lot of noise about how productive they are, but in reality, they can be ineffective when dealing with tasks.

Is Your Partner a Pessimist?

"I used to laugh when we first started dating because Jonah would always look at the very worst-case scenario. But as time went by, I began to get more and more depressed by his pessimistic outlook on life. If we planned a vacation, he would always say, 'We need to plan for if the weather gets rough, or one of us falls ill.' It sounds funny now, but I got to be terrified of going out on my father's boat. He would launch into lectures about how many lives were lost on boating lakes and how only strong swimmers could survive being tipped overboard. We had fire alarms everywhere and constantly watched news reports, watching for the bad news. If there were a disaster anywhere in the world, he would talk about it for hours. But the worst thing was that he repeatedly said that our relationship would probably end up in tears. So, it did in the end. He had the relationship anxiety, and I had the symptoms. It was on my way to see a therapist about my depression, and I had the sudden realization that my depression was in my own hands. I turned around, went home, and moved out." (Juli, age 29)

According to psychologists, pessimistic people expect things to be bad in most circumstances and events. Pessimists have poor mental and physical health; it can manifest in hostility toward life, depression, and heart disease. If you recognize the signs of a pessimistic tendency in your partner, then it's worth talking with him to discuss the possibility of therapy.

Does Your Partner Sabotage?

In a TED talk, psychology researcher Raquel Peel discusses her brush with self-sabotage:

> *"I assumed that people in my relationship would eventually leave me; I also assumed that all my relationships would fail." Peel says how she would "eventually pull the plug on romances whenever things got the least bit difficult." (Balerezo, 2019)*

If this sounds like your partner or the new love in your life, then don't expect things to run smoothly. Does your partner expect constant reassurance? Does he get anxious when things get serious?

Often, you may believe that it is you experiencing difficulty keeping the partnership going. You may ask yourself what is wrong with you. Perhaps you need to look at your new love very carefully. How defensive is your partner? How critical is she of some of the things you do? If your partner is not prepared to form a commitment or is not prepared to discuss long term goals, then this could indicate he has sabotage tendencies.

However, if you really -want this relationship

to last, then a loving conversation may be all that is required. Discuss with your partner how new relationships often create anxiety and that you sometimes feel the same. Suggest that you give each other time to grow into your relationship.

Take things slowly, and maybe your partner will overcome his relationship anxiety and want to protect the relationship rather than protecting himself.

Does Your Partner Doubt Your Love?

You really like this new guy in your life, and you can't help showing it. But you know deep down he is questioning your love for him. How do you know this? You recognize his patterns of behavior. His texts you, "Did you not receive my last text," because you did not reply immediately. Or perhaps he asks you – too often – what you are thinking.

There are many little "tells" that may alert you to the fact that your new lover is not secure. Unfortunately, it may be that he will always doubt your love for him, and if you are not cautious, you could end up fueling his doubts by constantly trying to convince him of your love. If you can't reassure him, then you may be in for an exhausting time.

KEY TAKEAWAYS

- Jealousy and possessiveness are destructive emotions. Recognize the early signs of control and the abnormal desire to share your social life outside of your relationship.

- Avoidant behavior can be hard to recognize. If the new love in your life is reluctant to make a commitment or is reluctant to begin a sexual relationship, *beware*. Some relationships can last years before avoidant behavior is recognized by a partner.

- If your partner is too clingy, then you must nip it in the bud. This desperate behavior by a partner can be exhausting, and you could end having to curtail some of your independence.

- Passive-aggressive behavior can be difficult to spot at first. They dislike being called to account and are likely to blame other people for what goes wrong in their lives. They can stonewall and make you feel guilty for not doing things well, when, in fact, they are the ones who are ineffective.

- You may recognize that your partner is pessimistic, but you may not recognize this as being relationship anxiety. Having a pessimistic outlook on life, seeing the glass as always half empty, can have a detrimental impact on your health and well-being. Being around people who always fear the worst is contagious. If you can't cheer your partner up under any circumstances, then your partner has relationship anxiety.

- How often has your partner sabotaged an event you were looking forward to? How often does he turn up late for family dinners? How often do you both make plans only for him to duck out at the last minute? Having these tendencies often relate to early childhood experiences or broken relationships that were never fully recovered from. You need to ask yourself if you have recognized these signs for a long time but have been reluctant to bring them out into the open. Now is the time.

- When your partner doubts your love for him, no matter how hard you try to show him you adore him, then he may never trust you – or the relationship. You need to have a conversation that brings these insecurities out into the open. Sometimes that is all that it takes.

Recognizing relationship anxiety in yourself and in your partner can serve you well, making you more aware of why your connections tend to break-down, and it can make you more empathic in the relationship you wish to nurture. This type of anxiety can have a huge impact on your life.

The following chapter discusses how living with anxiety can affect the way you relate to your partner.

CHAPTER FOUR
The Impact of Anxiety on Your Relationship

"I KNEW I WAS living with relationship anxiety. I didn't need my friends to point it out. But they did, just the same. To be honest, I was a kind of anxious person anyway in a generalized way. I worried about everything. My relationship was no different. But I began to notice how it impacted my relationship like I'd never noticed it impacting my life in general.

I suppose I just took it for granted I was a natural-born worrier. My relationship was different, though. I didn't want anything to go wrong, but from day one, I knew that my anxieties would get the better of my romance with Patrick. From the first moment we met, I had this overwhelming desire to be close to him. I placed my entire trust in him and looked to him for guidance and support in every aspect of my life. Looking back, it seemed like he was constantly trying to sort my life out. I found I couldn't make a decision without consulting him. When he showed signs of irritation, I got angry and reacted way *over the top. Fortunately, Patrick recognized my anxiety, and together we learned to combat my fears. While, deep down, I am always slightly anxious, my relationship with Patrick is still going strong, and last week Patrick asked me to marry him" (Judy, age 23)*

The impact of relationship anxiety can take many forms. Judy had to learn to deal with her natural desire to fret over the slightest thing. Many people do overcome their relationship fears and have rewarding relationships. But when anxiety gets in the way, it can affect your sex life, make you selfish, and make you socially isolate, not just you, but your partner as well. Relationship anxiety can also seriously affect your health and well-being.

Impact On Your Sex Life

Many of us experience anxiety over sex, especially in a new relationship. Maybe it is the first time for you, and you are inexperienced. Even if your first time goes well, you will feel anxious until you feel more secure in your relationship and with your own body. However, there could be more serious underlying anxieties impacting your sex life – and even hindering your sex drive.

Maybe you carry a bad memory of a sexual encounter that went wrong. Perhaps you ended up in a one-night stand, and you felt humiliated. Or perhaps your last experience of sex ended in dissatisfaction for both of you. Again, this is normal anxiety that will pass as you trust your partner more over time.

But maybe what you are bringing to your sex life is your early years' conditioning that did not encourage you to explore your own sexuality or encourage you to understand that sex is a normal part of adult life.

There are a variety of ways in which children are taught social expectations about sex; for women, the most relevant one is that sex is meant to be endured rather than enjoyed. Fortunately, this view is diminishing, and more women can now express their sexuality and explore their sex drive in an open and fulfilling manner.

Unfortunately, as women are becoming more sexually liberated, body image has become a big commercial factor in conditioning girls and women into believing they should look a certain way. Anxiety about body image can reduce sex drive, and it's not just women absorbing unrealistic views of what their bodies should look like.

Men can experience anxiety over their body image. While women may be concerned that their vaginas are the wrong shape or their breasts are too small/big, men have anxieties about the size of their penis.

If you or your partner have issues surrounding body image, they can be dispelled to a large degree by having a meaningful conversation. Discussing anxieties lovingly and sensitively, this common barrier to enjoying sex will disappear.

Selfish Behavior

Being self-absorbed generally means you are egotistical, self-obsessed, and selfish. This may come as a shock to those of us who have experienced being a little bit self-centered. After all, don't we need to take care of ourselves and be independent?

When facing difficult situations, we are advised to look inside, putting ourselves first for self-protection. However, when we assess our self-absorption, we need to ask ourselves whether our behavior towards a partner is built upon a selfish desire to ease our own anxieties. If you are placing self in the front of the line – to the exclusion of the feelings and needs of others – then your selfishness will almost certainly drive your partner away. It's likely to drive friends away, as well.

Psychologists believe that taken to this extreme, selfish behavior becomes narcissism. This manifests in lack of empathy and can easily turn a relationship into one of manipulation and a sense of entitlement.

Being selfish in a relationship never ends well. Experts believe that selfish behavior is a cover for feelings of anxiety and helplessness, a feeling that one will be "found out" that they are not as important or clever as people think. Dr. Leon Seltzer relates testimony of a woman recognizing that she is overly self-absorbed with her own anxieties:

"Nerves have a way of making you fold into yourself, obsessing over each awkward thing you've said or done in front of someone you're trying to impress.

*You're chatting away, but you're also very much
focused on you, trying to figure out the impression
you're leaving. Meanwhile, you've missed the last
five minutes of the conversation, which makes it
highly likely that the impression you're leaving is
that you're kind of a jerk."(Seltzer, 2016. p. 1)*

When you take this type of anxiety into a relationship, it can lead to you being inconsiderate, self-opin-
ionated, and manipulative.

Social Isolation

In basic terms, social isolation means being alone,
with no social interconnections. This may sound
strange when you may be experiencing relationship
anxiety. Social isolation differs from choosing to spend
some time in solitude to perhaps recharge your batter-
ies, meditate, or practice mindfulness.

The social isolation referred to in this section
describes the unhealthy isolation that stems from
relationship anxiety. First, the anxieties we have discussed so far can lead to individuals becoming socially
secluded. You may be possessive and perhaps jealous of
the social life your partner enjoys, and because of this,
you will slowly but surely erode your partner's outside
activities so you only have each other.

Marriage guidance experts believe this is a common
characteristic of failing marriages. When love first blossoms, it is only natural to want to spend all your time
with your new romance, and this may be by mutual

agreement. However, soon, you should both be resuming your social life independently or together.

Having relationship anxiety can lead to loneliness *within* your relationship, leading to anxiety and ill health. When searching for that one person to fill that empty space in your life, perhaps you are looking for someone – other than yourself – to fill that void. According to an article on *Time's* website: "28% of people who are dissatisfied with their family lives feel lonely all or most of the time." (Jalili, 2019. p.1)

What causes loneliness and social isolation in relationships? Psychologists believe that this comes about when people lose emotional connection to the important things – or people – in their lives. Partners drift apart. When a partner distances themselves, the other may experience social isolation because they no longer share the same friends or the same interests.

Relationship anxiety can create intense feelings of isolation and loneliness. If you feel alone in your relationship or you have lost friends and even family because of a controlling partner, then it is time to seek help from someone outside of the family.

Experts in relationship coaching can help you understand what contributes to your loneliness and help you to communicate more effectively with your partner so you can both regain some sense of companionship. Often, your partner may be experiencing this isolation, as well. However, if a partner is controlling your life, then it may be time to seek advice about separation or divorce.

To be clear about this, it is important to know where your feelings of isolation are coming from. Are you doing this to yourself or your partner because of insecurities you feel about your relationship?

For example, maybe your partner is comfortable telling you he loves you and is happy to share his life with you, and he wants you to have a social life too. Is your partner trying to tell you that your sense of loneliness and isolation is coming from within yourself? Are you too wrapped up in his and your lives you don't feel the need to socialize?

Still, you may sense within yourself discontent. Social isolation is a common theme that couples experience after the first glow of romance has cooled; unfortunately, this leads lonely and unfulfilled feelings in one or both partners.

Taking the Fun Out of Life

Often, we spend more time worrying about *things* than we spend *enjoying life.* This is common for all of us. We're concerned about our jobs, our parents' health, our own health, and our relationships. If you consider some issues discussed already throughout these chapters, you will realize that relationship anxiety impacts all aspects of our lives.

Let's take a little breather and think about what you may be worried about – and why. Are you concerned that you may not be compatible, but are heading into a long-term commitment anyway? He doesn't like the same things as you. You disagree about what movies to watch, and you differ over which restaurants you prefer.

Is this a problem, or are you just making it one? Everyone is unique, all raised by different parents with different outlooks on life. We may have gone to different schools and may have moved in different social circles. This is what makes us so exciting. Don't worry about the difference in likes and dislikes, enjoy the fact that each of you brings something new to the relationship.

Maybe you worry that the relationship won't last. Well, no one knows what lies ahead; the future hasn't been written yet! Enjoy your life with this person *now,* living in the moment rather than fearing for the future. Sometimes relationship anxiety makes us worry needlessly about what's ahead. You may assess your new partner too closely, when, in fact, you hardly know him. Perhaps you wonder if he is a responsible person, whether he will make a good father and whether he will take care of you in times of need.

Over time, you'll get to know this person and discover more about these character traits. Meanwhile, enjoy your new romance. No one knows what the future holds in store for us. Live responsibly, live mindfully, and enjoy the good times.

KEY TAKEAWAYS

- Relationship anxiety can ruin your sex life. It can inhibit you and distress your partner. Inhibitions about sex can color the way you share your bed. Learn to love your body and learn to trust your partner. Be prepared to explore your own sexuality and the expectations of your partner.

- Selfish behavior in relationships usually stems from insecurities deep within us. One serious complication of selfishness is that it stops you from recognizing narcissistic traits in you or your partner. Don't be blind to the psychological studies that look at the impact that selfishness has on a relationship. Learn more about yourself, and if you are a selfish partner, explore the reasons for this. Selfish behavior in a relationship usually ends badly for both partners.

- Social Isolation can stem from you experiencing relationship anxiety, or it can arise from deeply-rooted feelings of insecurity. Take care you are not imposing social isolation on yourself or your partner. It can lead to intense feelings of loneliness and despair.

- Relationship anxiety can frustrate your attempts to enjoy life. Feeling anxious all the time drowns out optimism and replaces it with dark fears. Let the sunshine in. Live for the moment, and don't fear the future; it hasn't happened yet. While you are sitting worrying, you are missing out on the laughter and fun that abounds around you.

Relationship anxiety can take a serious toll on your health and well-being, your capacity to have fun, and your willingness to surrender to the magic of a new love interest. The following chapter will discuss a variety of ways you can stop anxiety from damaging your relationship.

CHAPTER FIVE

Stop Anxiety from Sabotaging Your Relationship

It's Going to be Alright

IT IS GOING to be alright, and I'll tell you why. Because when you recognize what triggers your anxiety, you will be able to deal with it. While you may begin be experiencing exhaustion from your feelings of fear and *insecurity, you'll also begin listening to that small voice deep within rise to a roar of self-discovery. The more you learn about yourself, the more you will understand how past experiences shape future actions. You must drown out the critical voice and listen to the voice of mindfulness, self-development, and growth. If you really don't want to sabotage this relationship, **then don't**. Be kind to yourself, forgive yourself for past indiscretions (perceived or otherwise), and see what is good in your life. Knock your fears and anxieties out of the court. Start today." (The author)*

Listening to that critical voice inside, you can help to nurture your feelings of intimacy and warmth. It can help you to understand why your relationships end up on the garbage pile. By understanding yourself better, you will communicate your feelings more effectively. You will stop depending so on your partner's opinions and become more independent, growing into a calmer person, more in touch with both inner strengths and shortcomings.

Talk to Your Partner About Your Feelings

Talking about your emotions may be difficult for you. Often people with relationship anxiety are too stressed to talk about the way they feel; people find it hard to *listen,* too. You don't want to make a big deal of "the conversation," but at the same time, you need to be able to express your emotions.

This book has discussed how self-silencing can lead to ill health, even heart disease, and stroke. Getting things in the open often clears the air and brings people closer together. If you fear this connection is going south, don't let your partner brush you off, or let your words float around in the void as he continues texting or watching a baseball game. Choose the right moment.

A trick businesspeople and politicians use for getting their message across is *reinforcement.*

This requires that you use particular words to provide your partner with the information you feel is important. Here, it is how you are experiencing relationship anxiety. Make good eye contact and use encouraging words. Tell him how much you love him or how much you adore him, but keep in mind: the amount of adoration you fling at him needs to be tempered by how long you have known the guy! Don't scare him off by loading him down with your anxieties; simply let him know you are experiencing relationship anxiety but that you are working on it. Humor goes a long way when revealing your insecurities.

You don't want to appear flippant – or maudlin and self-absorbed – or he'll forget the conversation the second you leave the room.

Reflecting on your conversation will help you to internalize how you feel about revealing perhaps long-hidden emotions to your partner. Self-reflection is a positive way to become a more effective communicator, but it is not. about brooding, or having senseless conversations in your head. It's about recalling the focus of the conversation: what you said, how he responded.

Reflection also shows respect for your partner. It is used for thinking about how they responded, whether they offered reassurance or whether it made them feel a little insecure. This important thought process helps you better understand better the dynamics emerging as you move forward with your relationship.

Nurture Your Independence

The most common reason for wrecked relationships is becoming overly-dependent on a partner. How many of your friends seemed to disappear when they entered a new relationship? Friendship groups shatter, and social networks scatter. Oh, yes, you may keep in touch on social media, but things aren't the same anymore...until you get that call when the long-lost friend is looking up old acquaintances because the relationship hit the skids.

If you don't want this to happen to you, *nurture your independence*. Social media sites and blog articles abound with stories of how giving it all to a relationship led to abandonment and loneliness.

Being independent does not mean being selfish or careless with your partner's feelings. And it certainly doesn't mean you don't share a huge proportion of your time – at least initially – in each other's company. However, you were a whole person before you met; don't become a half-person (on non-person) to your family and friends. Maintain your independence.

In fact, defend it fiercely. If you enjoy going to the gym with friends a couple of nights a week, then continue with that, encouraging your partner to continue his friendships, as well.

Many women these days prefer to pay their own way when going out to dinner with their partner, especially before marriage or moving in together. Having your own car, your own bank account, and your own views and opinions all lead to a better relationship. It is not uncommon for men and women to keep their own apartments rather than move in with one another full-time.

This allows both of you to keep your own private space providing more control over your relationship.

If things get a little heated, as they often do in any relationship, cooling off can be done without drama, simply by stating that you need to spend some time at home. Consider the testimony of Sarah, who maintained her own apartment for five years during the first years of her relationship:

"Many of my friends would kid around about how my partner and I had our own apartments. We had made a commitment to each other, and we considered ourselves life partners. We didn't consciously decide to keep our apartments. We just sort of enjoyed our own space. Jack felt as much at home at my place as I did at his. Fortunately, we didn't live too far from each other, and we could actually walk to each other's homes. It made for some very romantic walks home to my place when it got late, and I wasn't staying at his place. Jack would accompany me home, and it always felt like a date night. Kissing goodnight at my doorstep, or his, might have seemed strange to our friends, but we both nurtured our independence, and keeping our own apartments was part of that. Eventually, when we decided to start a family, we set about buying our first home together. I confess that it was strange for both of us, but we were used to each other's independent ways, so the mutual respect we had developed over the years spilled over into our new lives together. We are still happily

together, now married with twins on the way"
(Sarah, age 37)

Being independent protects your relationship rather than fracturing it. Express yourself freely and honestly with your partner, creating the trust that mature relationships thrive on. Don't wreck your relationship by being overly dependent. Your partner should add something to your life, not take away from it; add something to his.

Meditation

When you bring anxiety into your relationship, you bring turbulence and noise. That noise may be in your own head, but it seeps out into the air around you. It permeates the very existence of your relationship, and you know without a doubt, that once again the relationship will suffer. For some time now, people have been turning away from medical help and relationship experts and embracing meditation as a way of calming a troubled mind.

Relationship anxiety doesn't exist in a vacuum; it's in every aspect of your life. You just cart it around with you everywhere you go, like a battered suitcase that goes with you from place to place. With each new relationship, out comes the suitcase and out comes the carefully packed-away anxiety. Meditation calms the mind and brings peace to the doubting voices in your head.

Anyone can meditate. It costs only a few minutes

of your time each day. Find a quiet place to sit or lie down comfortably. Gently close your eyes and concentrate only on your breath. Feel how you breathe. Take a deep breath, hold it for four seconds and then gently exhale; think only of the present. The past has gone, you can't change it. Just let it belong in the past.

The future isn't here yet; don't use your mental energy worrying about something that hasn't happened. Don't make up stories because that's all they are; stories written for the universe to read. As you slowly relax, just continue focusing on the moment. As you practice meditation, you will become better at it, and your moments of meditation will refresh, calm, and re-energize you.

Mindfulness gurus tell us that mediation is good for our health and well-being. It is a sure-fire way to dump that briefcase you pack so carefully every day. Meditation keeps us grounded in the present. So, if you constantly believe that you are going to wreck your relationship soon, change the story you're telling yourself about it.

This mind practice will help rid you of negativity; you will sleep better, be calmer, and have more control over your anxieties. Recognize your anxiety for what it is, just fear of the future – of the arrows you think are coming your way. Don't let anxiety define who you are. It's not you.

Smile and let it all go. We all allow our minds to wander, and many doctors believe that wandering minds bring more negative thoughts than positive ones, often leading to depression. Meditation concentrates the mind on *now,* teaching you to stay in the present moment because as your body relaxes, the "fight or flight" response eases, slowing down the heart rate and soothing anxiety.

Deliberate reflection and quieting of the mind teaches you how to love again, to understand your emotions and why you feel as you do. Heading into a relationship armed with a pocket full of calming thoughts and positive emotions is all you need.

Learning to Trust

If you don't know how to trust someone, it will surely spoil your relationship. Yes, you do need time to get to know someone before you begin divulging all your innermost fears and anxieties. We're all reticent to reveal personal things to people before we know we can trust them. However, if you have trust issues, you may never reach that point with a deserving partner.

A common worry is that the new partner may not like you, that you are not the perfect person you claim you are – or she acts like you are. Again, this is normal but at some point, you must relax and put your trust in the person you want to share your time and, perhaps, your life with. This can be difficult if your last relationship ended with your partner betraying you. Still, ask yourself why you find it hard to trust another. Have you always found it difficult to allow your defensive shield to drop? Have previous partners played around or treat you unkindly? Ask yourself what baggage you are bringing to the relationship.

Be open with your new partner, admitting you have trust issues and explaining (briefly) *why.* Share that you would like to take things slow to begin with. Sometimes it is easy to miss the signs that a partner will respect your trust; yet, consider how they respond when you make arrangements, such as dinner dates. Does he remember? Does he turn up on time? Does he respect your wishes when you don't want to do something? If not, these are clear signs that this person does not deserve your trust.

Dating Someone with Anxiety: What You Need to Do

Are You Really Listening?

This is not a facetious question. Many of us don't listen to other people talking because we want to do the talking. Good listening is a skill. If you are dating someone with relationship anxiety and you want to nurture this relationship, then you must learn to listen.

To learn more about the anxiety issues your new partner has, *ask,* and then have the courtesy of actually listening to their inner thoughts. This might sound like common sense but try it the next time someone is speaking to you. How often did your mind wander, or how often did you just wait for a pause in the conversation so you can jump into with your thoughts?

Are you sure you can actually recall the last

conversation someone had with you? Can you remember the essence of the conversation? Many of us can't because our minds are full of other things.

Be mindful when you discuss relationship anxiety with the person you are dating. Listen carefully, and don't just wait to hear something relevant about you. This conversation should be about him, not you.

Show empathy with your body language. Keep eye contact and nod your head encouragingly and mean it. Ask why you are having the conversation. Is it because you want to ease the anxiety felt by your partner, or is it because you want to know his secrets in order to judge him more closely? Consider that he may be astute enough to know this, and it's *why* he as anxiety issues.

Don't' zone out if he really opens up to you. Perhaps he has never had the opportunity before and relishes the opportunity to be more intimate about sharing his thoughts with you. You know what it feels like when people "go on too long," and we think "Now, I wish I hadn't asked," but ask you did, so pay attention. Sitting quietly (perhaps each with a glass of wine) is a perfect time to draw your date out. Listen carefully and empathize. You can do a lot to ease the anxiety someone might feel when striking up a new relationship.

Let that person know that they can trust you, that you will not kiss and tell or that you will not discuss his innermost secrets with your girlfriends.

Helping your date overcome their relationship anxiety takes maturity and skill, but if you don't want to spoil things with a person who is worth the trust you offer them, then it's worth showing how much you care.

Consider what journalist Helen Bala said about the time she spent listening to people's personal stories and the empathy she felt when being privileged to share people's deepest secrets.

> *"For a little over a year now, I've listened to strangers I meet on Craigslist tell me stories they've never told anyone before. I've interviewed someone who went through gender reassignment surgery and was falling in love for the very first time, as his true self. I've spoken with a man who lost his wife to alcoholism, struggling to rebuild a life without her. I cried when I spoke to a veteran who had lost both of his legs after serving two tours of combat abroad. My body shook with anger as I heard the confession of a father who had sexually abused his two daughters when they were young girls. I've heard stories about sexual abuse and mental illness, divorce and death, addiction and disability—stories that have left me in awe at the breadth and depth of humanity."* (Bala, 2015. p.1)

Setting Boundaries When Dating Someone With Relationship Anxiety

Setting boundaries is a good idea when you begin a new romance, but it's more important if you suspect you are dating someone with relationship anxieties. By establishing mutual boundaries, you are making it possible to feel secure and positive about each other. Right from the onset, you can frame your romance within a clear set of values, ideas, and limitations.

Anything goes is never a good idea when matters of the heart are concerned because people can take advantage of a heart blinded by love and/or passion. Boundaries are meant to be respected by both parties. Let's look at some examples.

If you don't wish your date to go through your purse or use your belongings without asking, then set that boundary, expecting it to be respected. If you wish to see friends on nights you are not with him, *see friends*.

If he objects, then that breaches your personal freedom. He should know these boundaries are important and should not be crossed. If your date expects you to meet up at short notice and this becomes a regular thing, then you need to set a firm boundary. You are not at his beck and call. Often people with relationship anxiety want constant reassurance they will not be dumped, so they impose their will on their partner by testing their feelings towards them.

If your date unexpectedly turns up at your door unexpectedly, this is a boundary issue. If your date wants to know why you were talking to that guy earlier, that is a boundary issue.

Boundaries should be put in place immediately if you suspect the person you are dating has relationship anxieties. Meaningful conversations can assuage many fears that a new partner may have about committing to a relationship. Be a good role model, showing interest in all that your date does, *without imposing yourself on them.*

Respect his boundaries as you expect him to respect yours, demonstrating that boundaries are there to keep you both secure and comfortable. You both know where you stand, so there is no second-guessing.

Often, people with relationship anxieties feel more secure with boundaries in place. They recognize their own anxieties and may fear they will cross the lines that will bungle the relationship. Having boundaries fortifies, rather than weakening. If the person you are dating becomes a regular item in your life, some of these boundaries will naturally lessen as a more open relationship begins.

71

KEY TAKEAWAYS

- Remember that it will be alright in the end. You don't have to spoil every relationship you have. Learn to recognize your anxieties and address them slowly but surely. We all suffer from anxieties when we embark on a new relationship, so recognize them for what they are. Be positive and know that anxiety is a normal response to your fear of the unknown. Knock your demons down, and you come out stronger and happier.

- Learn to communicate with your partner. Be prepared to open up. Talk to your partner about your anxieties. He probably is anxious too! Take the time to learn about each other. It's one of the most rewarding aspects of a new relationship.

- Nurture your independence. Stay true to yourself and don't give up your personal freedoms; no relationship is worth it. Remember that by nurturing your independence, you are respecting your partner's independence too.

- Take the time to meditate every day. Be present. Practice living in the moment and enjoy what you have. Relationship anxiety can be managed by making meditation part of your everyday routine.

- Learn to trust your partner. Recognize the emotions within yourself and inside your own head that make it hard for you to trust people.

Notice the things that your partner does to assure you of his trust. Don't look for perceived wrongdoing on his part.

- Dating someone with relationship anxieties? Learn to listen to his fears. Show him it's time to trust you with his feelings. Show empathy and kindness.

- Remember to set clear boundaries if you are dating someone with relationship anxieties. It is easy to fall prey to the needs of others, especially in a new relationship, when love, lust, and passion, all cloud your judgment.

Dating is fun, it's exciting, and anyone can tell you that new love in your life changes how you view the world. You really do hear birds singing and bells ringing. New love takes your breath away. But if you are dating with anxiety, that romantic picture can change to one of uncertainty and fear. The following chapter discusses how to manage dating with anxiety.

Don't Forget to Claim:
YOUR FREE BONUS - 30-Days of Relationship Affirmations eBook!

As a way of thanking you for your purchase, I have a **free bonus** to offer you.

In addition to the information already provided in this book, I have created the *30-Days of Relationship Affirmations* eBook which provides you with 30 ready-made daily relationship affirmations. These will help you overcome any relationship roadblocks and strengthen your mind so that you can enjoy a more loving and intimate relationship.

Click (or tap) below to get your FREE Bonus instantly.

Click here:

www.mangobroom.com/relationship-affirmations/

CHAPTER SIX
Dating with Anxiety

"*OH, MY GOODNESS. When I started dating again, I was so nervous. Looking back, I'm not even sure how I found the nerve. I so wanted to get on with my life, and I wanted to have some fun. I had been with my previous guy for over five years. We were soon to be married. Suddenly he got the opportunity to work in Germany for an unspecified time, and I just couldn't make a move. We decided to break up, and it broke my heart. Then another eight months went by before I started to feel I was missing out, and I had so much love to give. But I was filled with guilt that I'd let my man just walk out of my life. I was scared that I might do it again when it came to making a commitment.*

My friends thought I was too hard on myself and that perhaps more underlying issues caused the breakup. To be honest, this just made it worse; it was just something else to worry about. What underlying problems? How could I not know about these things?

I am now happily single and would tell anyone who

finds returning to the dating game too nerve-wracking to take a long deep look at yourself. What do you want out of your life? What are your ambitions, hopes, and dreams? Find the answers to these questions, and when the dating starts, you know exactly what you want and, more importantly, what you don't want." (June, age 26)

A return to dating can be daunting, especially if it's been a long time or you have experienced a bad break-up, but the fact that you are wondering if it's time to get out there tells you that the time is now.

Start Dating Again

Dating again can seem quite intimidating, especially if you have been away from the dating scene for a while – but people do it all the time. Divorced people date again after being out of the market for years.

Perhaps you have been busy following your career and remained celibate for a while. It's quite easy for friends to give you this advice. People jump back into the dating pool every day and never regret it; you just must overcome your anxiety.

But this is much easier than it sounds. *What if I make the wrong choices? What if I fall madly in love, and he hates me? Isn't it easier just to stay single?* Well, no, because you want to date again, so accept that it will be daunting and sit back and enjoy the ride.

The first thing to do: forget the past. This is a new

you and a new him. Don't carry your personal baggage into your next relationship. He just won't want to carry it with you or on your behalf. Don't go out on a rebound; it never works because you will find the things that your partner wasn't and overlook the things you admire in a person. Perhaps, like June, you might be tempted to date a man who is a little stoic and un-ambitious. He won't run off to start a new life in a European city. Yet. is this what June wants? Only June knows that because she must take time for self-evaluation about her life before she takes the plunge again.

Self-evaluation allows you to discover a new you that may be hidden inside. You must decide if your fear is greater than the 'you' that's stirring inside, the 'you' that's looking for excitement and emotional fulfillment. Allow yourself to begin again. It's going to be alright. Permit yourself to go out on a date. Don't wait around for someone to set you up on a blind date; go, have some fun. That date will find you.

Don't wait around until you discover what the current "dating rules" are, either. Do what you feel is right. Feel your way. Trust your intuition. A good way to begin is to explore different settings. Go to the theatre, night clubs, yes, by all means, consider a respectable dating app as an acceptable way of meeting new people. If that turns out to NOT be your thing, start a new hobby, and let everyone know you are on the market again. Finally, don't rush into dates just because someone asked you out. Take things slowly and be choosy about who you date. It is all out there, so go get it!

How to Overcome Dating Anxiety

Most dating websites affirm that dating anxiety is quite common; why wouldn't it be? You are meeting someone for a first date. You are hoping to strike up a relationship, but the problem is you are so wrapped up in your own anxieties you know you just won't enjoy the experience. The evening goes by in a whirl of awkward silences of embarrassed laughter and downright terror if he asks you for more than a good-night kiss.

It need not be like this. You can overcome your anxiety if you prepare properly and don't be hard on yourself. Think about what your anxiety – what's that all about? The most common feeling of dread is saying things you didn't want to – or mean to – say. For example, when you are anxious, you might find yourself saying idiotic things just to make conversation. "Did it take you long to get here?" And you can hear that voice in your head saying, *What a stupid question!* How's he going to respond to that, especially when you already know he lives just a couple of blocks away? What you really wanted to say was, "Have you lived in this neighborhood long"?

It's likely that this open-ended question will elicit a lengthy response, long enough, at least for you to break the ice and start a meaningful conversation. When the conversation really gets going, and he asks you questions about your job and the neighborhood where you live, you may begin to get cautious. *Why is he asking me questions?* Do you edit your answers to avoid giving too much away?

You may realize that you want him to like you, but you can't just agree with everything he says and laugh at all his jokes because you think you will come across as being needy. Well, enough already. It's time to overcome these fears.

There is absolutely nothing wrong with preparing a few open-ended questions. Try to avoid yes/no answers; they can leave awkward silences. For example, if you are eating out, you can ask, "What is your favorite food to eat at this restaurant?" That's much better than asking if they serve fish.

If you prepare some questions, you are more likely to feel in control. Remember, too, that everyone enjoys talking about themselves; if there is an awkward pause in the conversation, you can ask your dinner date about themselves. For example, "If you could steal a day off work and watch Netflix all day, what would you watch?" Or, "If you had the chance to live in a shack in the Amazon jungle for six months, would you do it?"

Light-hearted humor is the best way to overcome dating anxiety. Don't pass your anxiety onto your dinner date; it will result in long, awkward silences. Picture that cool person you are deep inside and present that image.

Don't present that wild, chaotic person who lives inside your head. Be the person you want to be, not the person he wants you to be. Dating anxiety does not just go away; it fades with practice. The more you practice calm, the calmer and less anxious you will become.

Seven Ways to Begin Dating
When You Have Anxiety

1) Accept You are Anxious

Blogger Alison Barron had this to say about dating anxiety, which sums up what it feels like to be out there feeling scared and vulnerable.

> *"Explaining to my significant other that I have anxiety is difficult, but admitting I'm panicking at the moment is far harder. Opening up to God is easy for me because God will never let me down. But with another person, especially one I'm interested in being intimate with, my initial reaction is to hide my anxiety. What if it scares him off? What if he can't handle the fact that our relationship stresses me out, even if it's healthy and I'm happy? Of course, if the answer to those questions is "It will scare him off" and "He can't handle it," then maybe it's better off that I know sooner rather than later since anxiety and I am a packaged deal." (Barron, 2020. p.1)*

This is everyone who begins dating again! It's tough, but perhaps honesty is the best policy. Open up, say you are anxious and it's been a while since you dated. If you say this with enough confidence (perhaps a contradiction in terms), you will either scare him out the door, or he'll admit that he is anxious too.

You need not come across as a pathetic jiggering idiot; you just have to say. "Gee, I have been really anxious about this date tonight." If he doesn't take the bait and tell you he's anxious too, then perhaps he isn't worth your anxiety.

2) Talk About It

If your date shows enough interest, talk about what anxiety does to you. You can make this humorous, like the way you get your coat sleeve caught up indoor handles, or wandering around aimlessly trying to find the lady's room because you don't want to push through the crowds at the bar to ask someone. Don't hope to have a deep and meaningful conversation. This can turn out badly, with perhaps your date heading for the restroom and *not coming back*.

Keep conversations light and ever so slightly silly. "How would you react if someone sneaked into your apartment and painted everything black, including your furniture?" Actually, the sillier your questions, the less he will notice your nervousness. Laughing a lot on a first date is so refreshing, and the time will fly by.

You will be amazed at how much you can discover your date by being whimsical. Save the flirtation for another time. Take things slowly. Being flirty can get you into deep water. If your date responds by coming on too heavy, you will want to leave. So, hold back the flirty signals until you know more about him.

3) Embrace the Fun

Make this a fun time. Don't take yourself – or your first dates – too seriously; it will only serve to pile on the anxiety. Yes, things can go wrong. You might discover that your date has turned out to be a jerk. But hey, as long as he does you no harm, just go with the flow and have a good time. Meeting new people should be fun. Yes, I know you spent four hours at the beauty parlor and spent a fortune on that dress, but that's all part of the fun. If you have unrealistic expectations, it just adds stress to an already stressful proposition. A nice romantic candlelit dinner may be fine with someone you are gradually falling in love with, but a first date – even a second date – can be awkward if you are not ready for that commitment.

Dance, dine, walk in the rain, watch afternoon movies but do them expressly to have fun. It all goes back to being mindful. Don't worry about tomorrow, don't fret about past disasters – just enjoy the here and now. If you are practicing mindfulness, a first date is an ideal opportunity to immerse yourself in the present. Know what is going on around you, notice how your date pays attention (or not) to what you say. Taste the food in your meal. Be present, and your evening will be a perfect combination of adrenaline rush and tranquility.

4) Take it Slow

Take things ever so slowly. Maybe you have not been on the dating scene for a while and you are acutely aware that you'll be doing something different and new. This thought can make you anxious. *What am I doing here? Go home. This is bound to end in disaster, or worse, deep humiliation.*

Acknowledge that you are anxious, and this feels new. Take a few deep breaths and order a bottle of wine. Hide behind the menu for a couple of minutes till you quiet your nerves. Unless your date has ordered a table, try to sit in an area that is a little noisy.

A good way to adjust back into the dating pool is to choose the venue yourself, in an environment where you are not necessarily on your best behavior. For example, a dinner date may be quite stressful: what to wear, what not to eat (spaghetti comes to mind), who pays the bill, etc. Even eating in front of a stranger can be awkward sometimes. Instead, consider meeting over coffee or drinks. Chatting is easier when you are not eating, and you can always make your excuses and leave early if you feel the evening may be a disaster. Stay in control and accept that you are nervous, as everyone is on first dates.

5) Don't' Use Your Ex as an Excuse

If you are willing to discuss your anxiety to a new date, then a general rule of engagement is that you don't blame your ex for your own shortcomings. It is a negative way to begin a relationship.

Often, when on a first date, the subject of the "ex" comes up, and while it may seem like a good icebreaker, bad-mouthing your ex when they are not there to defend themselves says more about you than it does about him/her. Be generous and leave your ex in the past where they belong. Try not to use an ex as an excuse to cut short an evening out with a new date, either.

For example, we all have common traits; if your date says or does something that reminds you of your ex, this doesn't mean he *is* your ex. Do not reject a new friend because he does something that your past lover did – something you didn't like. If you like other things about this fellow, then just relax and have a good time. Be curious about their life and explore the possibilities of getting to know someone new.

6) Be Ready to Duck Out

Occasionally, you realize that you have made a mistake when agreeing to date someone. Be prepared for this. It is all about how much you can take control of a new situation, and that's why an informal date is often better than a dinner date or a night at the theatre; those venues make it so much harder to make your excuses and leave early. Also, make sure you can get home alone if you need to. Don't, choose venues not easily accessible to taxis if you are not using your own car.

So, there you are, sitting in a cozy bar sharing a nice bottle of wine. You get a feeling this date is not going too well. It not unusual for people to arrange for a friend to call them in the evening to check how things are going, providing a good time for either of you to say, "I'm sorry, I have to leave."

In another case recently, a man and woman, having first met online, were now meeting in person for the first time. Two friends sat at a nearby table to ensure that the woman was genuine and not trying to trick him into anything. Naturally, these are worst-case scenarios, and once you are back in the swing of things, dating will feel more normal, and you will have fun.

7) Go with the Crowd

First dates need not be stressful. If you find it difficult to calm your dating anxiety, get back into the market by accepting invitations from friends and family. Barbecues, hiking trips, parties, weddings, beach days, and holiday get-togethers should all be on your list of things to do. Couples often meet at such events, so why not use these as first dates?

If you have an event coming up, and someone invites you on a date, ask them to join you at an informal event such as a party or a hiking event. If they agree to this, anxiety can be easier because it is a casual occasion. Other venues, such as singles holidays, are also a good way of meeting new people. Be brave but be cautious. Use your anxiety to its best advantage. Our anxieties are there for a purpose sometimes; trust your instincts and stay safe.

KEY TAKEAWAYS

- Dating anxiety is a normal experience. It can be particularly stressful if you have been away from the dating scene for a long time, or you have experienced a bad break-up. Acknowledge that you feel anxiety, but remember that life is for living, not for regret. Get out there and have some fun.

- There are many ways to overcome dating anxiety. Talking about your anxiety to a new date can be a good icebreaker if you can joke about it a little.

- Prepare open-ended questions in advance to fill awkward silences but make them fun hypothetical questions. A first date is not the time for soul-searching.

- There are lots of ways you can approach the dating scene if you have been away from the action for a while. Talk about your anxiety, embrace the fun in meeting a new person, take things slow and easy, don't use your ex to score points with your new date, be ready to duck out if you need to, and look for informal ways to begin dating, meet at crowded venues such as beach parties, outdoor pursuits, and single holidays.

Of course, no one denies dating can be stressful, but it shouldn't prevent you from pursuing a well-rounded social life that embraces the dating game. Once your romance takes off, you will wonder why you were ever so anxious. However, it's never always smooth sailing. One of the most destructive influencers in terms of relationship anxiety is social media. The following chapter explores the impact of social media on your important connections.

CHAPTER SEVEN
Social Media

"I AM REALLY HAPPY *in my relationship with my partner. I think we are really compatible. We don't earn an awful lot of money between us, but we manage to go out and socialize occasionally, and we are saving to rent an apartment in the city. The trouble is that my social media friends seem to be getting their lives together much better than we are. Their Instagram photos leave me so envious of their lifestyles. There are always photographs of beautiful bouquets of flowers bought for birthdays and Valentine's, little gifts they have bought for each other and romantic vacations in Europe. I try to make my life with my partner as beautiful as I can, but we spend most of our time struggling to get through the week on long hours at work and poor pay at the end of the month." (Jen, age 22)*

This is a common problem for people today. Every little thing ends up on social media and is seen by friends and work colleagues. Judgments and comparisons of lifestyles are inevitable and can result in immense dissatisfaction in our lives and in our relationships. So, how much damage can social media have on your romantic relationship?

The Social Media Effect

Social media can cause your relationship anxiety to flare up, especially if you are a huge fan of the many sites. There has been wide-world research into the impact that social media is having on peoples' lives.

With the rise of accounts such as Twitter, Facebook, and Instagram, the way people communicate with each other has altered dramatically. How people maintain friendships has changed too, but one of the biggest changes lies in the way romantic relationships are created and sustained. Many studies have reported that the effect on romantic relationships increases relationship anxiety and, on the whole, has a negative impact; a common culprit is jealousy.

A recent survey was conducted using the "The Social Network Site Intrusion Questionnaire (SNSIQ)," that asked university students about their views on social media and how it impacted their relationships. Negative responses included participants who blamed social media sites for problems with their romantic partners, citing many reasons for relationship anxiety and breakups with their partners. Other research projects support this finding of significantly higher anxiety levels from those engaging regularly in social media, and most participants relayed that they experience real difficulties engaging with people *offline*.

Being Present

Think about when you get together with your friends. You immediately place your phone on the table, indicating that you are not entirely focused on them. If your phone rings or you get a Facebook notification, you'll answer it, regardless of who you are with. Long gone are the days of getting irritated by someone answering their phone; now people accept such intrusions as a matter of course and accept it as normal behavior. If you take your eyes off your cell phone for a moment while in a restaurant or a bar, you will see most people checking their cells' social media sites or email/messaging.

This phenomenon is known as "phubbing," which means to snub someone when choosing to look at your phone instead of them. The fact is that social media use can – and does – spill over into personal relationships, with couples complaining that it has an impact on their romantic relationship. If you are going on a date night, put your cell phone on silent, leave it in your pocket, and don't look at it. Whether your date will do the same is in the lap of the gods.

Relationship Anxiety and Social Media

Many young people have admitted there is a noticeable difference in the way they and their partners behave when they have been on social media for any length of time. One young woman reported in a questionnaire that both she and her partner seemed more on the edge and anxious after long periods spent on social media sites. She also added that they argued more.

The reason for so much research in recent years is an attempt to understand exactly what happens when we engage with social media sites. Can you imagine a time when people received love letters and snapshots attached to handwritten notes, and young lovers waited for hours just for that special person to telephone them on the house phone? Many older people are familiar with the song Pennsylvania 6-5000 (Glen Miller) where a husband called his wife from a famous hotel in Manhattan.

Some will argue that communication has improved since those days and improved for the better. This aspect of social media will be discussed further on, but meanwhile, there is little doubt that social media engagement has created anxiety in romantic relationships.

According to Lianna Tsanarides, LCSW, there are over 1.8 billion active users on Facebook and an "average American has an average of 5 social media accounts" (2018, p.1) This is phenomenal, but it does not explain why it has such a negative impact on romantic relationships. The sad fact is that people have a tendency only to post positive things going on in their lives. You want to update your social media when you change your relationship status from "single" to "in a relationship," but as the saying goes, no one wants to know what sad Sally or Sid is crying about now.

Unfortunately, many relationships have abruptly ended by one partner seeing an unexpected changed status on their partners' social media. And that's just the beginning. Relationship anxiety can flare up when you compare your own relationships with those of others. How do you feel when your friend's partner buys her a car or takes her on a fabulous vacation? The photographs are wonderful, and they've never looked happier, and then you find yourself arguing with your partner about which movie to watch on Netflix.

Often relationships suffer because one or the other partner spends far too much time on their cell phones. If this is you, perhaps you need to think carefully about why you are doing this. Is this an avoidance strategy? Does your partner bore you, or is this just a habit you have developed?

If your partner feels ignored because you are on social media all the time, perhaps they are right. But perhaps you are just filling up the time because your partner is watching sports on TV and you don't wish to. Tensions can arise when this happens. You can be accused of not sharing your partners' hobbies and activities. This can be problematic because texting and sending funny GIFs while your partner has set up the TV for a night of sport sort of indicates that you are not interested. Interestingly, reading a book or a magazine does not seem to elicit the same reaction.

Sharing Your Romantic Relationship with Others

One reason your partner may object to you constantly being on social media is that it feels like you are sharing your relationship with others. In other words, your friends go with you everywhere in your apartment or house! You communicate with your friends from the most personal places, including the toilet and the bathtub. Your friends are with you all the time, and what your partner may ask is, "*Why aren't you here with me?*" Think about this for a moment. Imagine you feel very lonely. Perhaps you are new in town, and you haven't struck up any friendships yet. Imagine too that you have no cell phone. If you take a bus journey downtown on a crowded bus, are you still lonely?

Well, you are because you don't know the people you are sharing the bus with. This is what like being with someone who is constantly glued to their social media. This is what can cause relationship anxiety for your partner. Consider how social media can cause your relationship to falter.

Stop Comparing Relationships on Social Media

How would you react if your best friend argued with their partner on Facebook? The messages fly backward and forwards instantaneously. The written abuse heightens as the minutes tick by. Are you horrified and turn your cell phone off because it feels like you are intruding, or do you avidly scroll down?

Maybe you're fascinated and unable to stop scrolling, much like witnessing a car crash, something uncommon and unpleasant that you can watch from afar. What's common is the reverse of this scenario. Everyone looks perfect. Photos of your friends with their significant others smile beautifully against iconic monuments such as the Eiffel Tower or the Taj Mahal. No one posts anything resembling everyday life. Even food photos are presented in a good light on Instagram, so romantic relationships are bound to get the star treatment.

It's so easy to present a wonderful view of your life, and it's so easy to hide mental anguish and depression behind a smiling selfie. While you are comparing your life to someone else's, remember that *that someone else* could be grappling with sad issues in their life.

Stop comparing your romance to others'. It causes relationship anxieties, depression, and breakups with partners. Having images of perfect lives constantly around you will inevitably make you believe that is normal, and your life isn't. So, you wind up trying to make it perfect, and of course, you fail because *life isn't like Photoshop*. Maybe you criticize your partner because they don't rise to your expectations of a perfect partner. Perhaps you even start to believe that your relationship isn't working.

Social media always presents a perfect image, so it's absolutely no use trying to compete. You may be struggling with a broken relationship, and there is your best friend social posting orchestrated images of their recent engagement or wedding. To give this some perspective, people have shared their family photos with friends since the invention of the camera. This is a normal activity, and sometimes you may feel envious or a little sad that you are not the one getting engaged or married or being proposed to.

Most of the time, you are likely pleased with your friends and family when they share photos of precious moments. So, why is social media different? It is different because you are now bombarded with images of happy times, handsome men kissing happy smiling women, hugging charming children, and perfect pets. You are viewing perfect happy people in happy relationships but 24-hours a day! And, of course, you push the 'like' button whether you like the image or not. According to research, pushing that like/happy/love button happens millions of times every day, becoming almost compulsory.

So, what happens if you post an image of you and your new partner and you get no likes? Are you a failure? This behavior can only be seen as unhealthy. It plays havoc with our moral compass, and it plays havoc with our relationships.

Together Against a Social Media World

It's time to stop the comparisons. You are unique, and so is your partner. You don't require validation from social media. You should be proud of your achievements, and be proud of each other. The urge to post happy photos is probably too entrenched in all of us to stop doing this, but if you continue with your social media accounts, then you must stop comparing your life to others.

Only you know what lies behind that smiling couple you posted on social media. Only you know your personal hardships and anxieties. It is the same for everyone else. Together you and your partner have your own expectations and goals in life. Demand to stay up close and personal – but only with your partner, your family, and your closest friends. It's enough to know that relationship anxiety can get the better of all of us from time to time, without the added anxiety of immersing yourself in unrealistic expectations of what your relationship should look like.

Seven Quick Tips to Overcome the Social Media Effect

1. Have clear guidelines. These could include no cell phones in play when watching movies together or at dinner.

2. Keep your phone in your purse or pocket. Agree when you are out on a date together that cell phones will not be on display.

3. Do not respond to calls on your cell phone when spending time together unless you can see on the display it is urgent (a family member, for example.)

4. Agree to set time limits on how much time you spend on social media during a day.

5. Do not go on social media sites during the night, even if you can't sleep.

6. Decide whether it's time to deactivate your

social media accounts for a while so you can reconnect with what is going on around you.

7. When out together, resist the urge to take selfies that you immediately post on social media.

Living with Social Media

One thing is for certain; social media will not go away. Therefore, you need to learn how to live alongside it without it taking over your life and distorting your perceptions of life. Again, be proud of your achievements, your family, and your good friends. Taking photographs and, now, videos of significant events in your life is important and is a historical account of passing time.

However, like many technological advancements in today's world, we need to use social media with caution, or at the very least, with humor. Your reality is important – warts and all. As you scroll down your account, remember that although you may think nothing of it, the images are creating pathways in your brain that contribute to false perceptions. This means you are more likely to make false judgments about people based on what images you are presented with. This is the kind of intrusion that would have been unheard of a few years ago.

Social media is not all bad if it is used with thought. It has some well; people who may be shy and awkward or those who may have difficulty making friends have found an outlet in social media. Used with maturity, social media can extend people's view of the world and connect people from across the world who might not otherwise meet or learn about different cultures and traditions.

Also, in a world where families can be scattered across the globe, the Internet brings loved ones together in ways we never imagined possible. Long-distance relationships can be nurtured until such a time you are together again. There is so much you can gain from being connected with the world. Using it to make judgments about people and comparing your life to theirs is using social media in a negative and addictive manner, which will only create more relationship anxiety in your life.

KEY TAKEAWAYS

- Social media can cause your relationship anxiety to flare up.

- Don't compare yours and your partner's relationships with others on social media.

- Comparisons can play with your emotions making you jealous and discontented.

- Using social media when you are in someone's company is called "phubbing" - which means you are snubbing your companion/s by engaging with others on social media.

- Making comparisons of social media leads to low self-esteem, anxiety, and depression.

- Live with social media responsibly and have clear guidelines about when you are on social media and when you will not be.

- Ensure that your cell phone is not on display on date nights or in the bedroom.

Maintaining a loving relationship takes time and effort. Overcoming relationship anxiety is a big part of maintaining the beautiful relationship you strive for. Using social media wisely and being present in your relationship will manifest great rewards. Discover how to maintain (or even rekindle) the flame that makes a beautiful relationship.

CHAPTER EIGHT
A Beautiful Relationship

"MANY PEOPLE ASK me how come my partner and I are so happy together. Well, the truth is it wasn't always the case. It was wonderful at the start of our relationship. We got married and settled down. We have two small children who make our lives hectic. Over the years, we seemed to disconnect somehow. I was busy with the children, and he was busy with work. We seemed to live on two different planets. Then we started to bicker with others over the smallest things. We always made up, but it started to worry me. Where had the magic gone? Then I started reading articles on how to rekindle your love, and it struck me like a lightning bolt. We hardly ever did the things we used to, and we rarely ever took the time to sit down and really talk to each other. It took a while, but gradually, having admitted to each other that we were just coasting along, to reassess what we loved about each and the journey to our rekindled love began just there." (Paula, age 42)

Over time, it is easy to fall into the trap of taking each other for granted. You drift apart without even being aware of it. You don't make love as often as you used to, and you blame your busy lives for that. The romance fades as you grapple with work, home, and family. But love can be rekindled, and the following sections show you can do it.

Rekindle the Spark

Taking a Walk Down Memory Lane

Marriage guidance experts report that one of the most common reasons couples seek counseling is that they seem to have drifted apart and are contemplating separation or divorce. Therapy does help, but there are lots of self-help tools to get the spark ignited again.

First, you both need to remind yourself why you fell in love in the first place. What was it that attracted you to each other? Of course, it may initially have been chemistry and lust, but that's okay. What did you do when you were not in bed? Think about where you were when you met and what you were doing. Try to conjure up those first moments when you met. How did you feel? Hold on to those feelings. Put some time aside and plan on taking a romantic walk. If you need a babysitter, then get one. Walking in the park at twilight can be magical, and you may have forgotten what it feels like to walk hand-in-hand through the park or by the river. Remember what you did on your very first date. Did you have fun? Did you go to a movie or dinner? Try to recreate the feelings you had when you looked into the eyes of the person you eventually spend your life with.

Cultivate New Hobbies Together

A recent study of romantic love suggests that cultivating new hobbies together can rekindle the flame. (Mayer Robinson, 2020, p.1)

Often, couples just get stuck in their routine lives and continue to engage in activities they have long tired of. If this is you, then it's time to move on. Find something else more exciting and sign up for it together. If you are prepared to go out on a limb and do something crazy that you've never done before, you will be amazed at how much energy you have for rekindling that spark. Try to indulge your senses and do something exhilarating like climbing a mountain, hang gliding, or how about trying one of the newer activities such as booking an escape room adventure?

If neither of you is really into scary things, why not book a few tennis lessons or something calmer, like fishing. The idea is that you do something together that you have never done before. Learning new things can be fun, and when you begin laughing out loud, you have begun the journey to rekindling those very first feelings of love. Take the time to think about what made your heart fill with joy the first few times you got together with your partner. Those feelings are still there; you just need to breathe new life into them. Scientists believe that when you do exciting things, your body releases dopamine, which gives you a sense of exhilaration. Share that experience.

Skin on Skin

There is nothing more powerful than feeling your partner's hand in yours. When was the last time that occurred? Remember that first touch. When you have a moment, perhaps when you are watching a movie together or cuddled up in bed, just reach for your partner's hand, and gently stroke it, explore the contours, feel the sensation of skin on skin.

Many couples forget the importance of everyday touching. For many couples, the only time they kiss or touch each other sensually is when engaging in foreplay, or as an invitation to making love. Once more, science responds to this by saying that demonstration of affection, such as kissing, stroking, and holding another person in your arms, boosts your immune system and releases powerful happiness hormones.

You can do this anytime you wish. Shows of affection, such as touching and kissing, go a long way in rekindling the romance in your relationship. This doesn't mean you have to be serious about this. Nibbling your partner's ear while he is making coffee or reading a book can be unexpectedly pleasurable. Walking past your partner in a sexual manner and whispering endearments are fun things to do. If you have teenage children and they start complaining that you should "get a room," you'll know you've begun rekindling that flame.

Crazy Kind of Love

For a while, forget the mundane responsibilities of earning a living, raising children, making a home, and think about all the crazy things you can do together, *if* you take the time out of your busy schedules to do so. Are you brave enough to do silly things? While no one is suggesting you jaywalk or knock on people's doors and run away, there are lots of things you can do together to reignite love and touch base with your inner child. It should be your sort of crazy, or else it doesn't work.

Think about Holly Golightly (Breakfast at Tiffany's,) when they wore those silly masks. How romantic was that! What about the bouquet of sharpened pencils from the movie, You've Got Mail? Okay, they're chic movies, but who says you have to act all grown-up every second of the day? If you think about it, there are lots of fun things you can do together that cost little and can be done spontaneously. Even a ride through the park on bicycles is a fun thing to do. The trick is that you do them together: that you take the time to do these things without being encumbered by children and the weight of responsibility.

Time to Talk

In the previous chapter, the discussion focused on social media. It is pertinent in this chapter too. Develop the art of conversation, consciously talking to each other. Re-visit what your partner feels and thinks about things. Ask him or her what they need to be happy, whether past ambitions remain in their hearts. Talk to each other about your hopes and your fears as you reach this juncture in your lives.

How do you each feel about the future? What are your greatest fears? How often do you hear your partner, but don't listen? How often do you say, "I don't have the time at the moment, we'll talk later," but you never do? How much do you keep hidden from your partner?

Yes, serious conversations are needed and expected in a relationship, but conversations don't always need to be serious. While you are sitting quietly, while no one is around to disturb you, inject some fun into your conversation. Ask each other hypothetical questions and make silly observations. Talk, laugh, and touch: three magic words.

Connecting with the One You Love

Connecting with the person you love is making the spark that will ignite the flame that may have died down as you have trodden life's journey together. Here's a romantic poem written by D. Yearwood, (2020):

The Connection We Have:
Every moment we've spent together,
has touched our lives, our souls forever.
The things we share, the things we've done,
and the permanent things we can't undo.
The person you are, heart and soul,

came to life, with emotion, desire and passion.
Because of you, I'm full of love
It's all your fault, I'm loving you like this.
We've connected, wide and deep,
no one can remove, this connection we have.
Our feelings are blended, never to be undone,
A part of me will always be you.
A part of you will always be me,
no matter what happens, that much is certain
our souls are one, till that moment comes.
I will love you forever.
I will love you forever,
for worse or for better,
You are tattooed in my heart,
nothing can tear, our souls apart.
You'll always be mine,
with love and honesty, only for you.
Source: http://www.lovelifepoems.net/
love-poem/the-connection-we-have

What does it mean to feel connected to your partner? If you consider the words of the poem above,
there are clues there. What is the connection you feel?
Can you feel a mutual bonding of love between you?
If not, you can reconnect on ways you perhaps never
imagined. A question that many individuals ask when
contemplating their relationship is whether he or she

considers the relationship important enough to invest effort in making it better.

Often people in relationships grapple with the notion that there should be more to your relationship than which is evident in your daily lives. Perhaps it's time to sit down and think about what kind of connections you wish to nurture. Maybe you want to connect more physically, and certainly, the previous sections can guide you towards doing that. Do you wish to connect on a more spiritual or emotional level? Maybe it's all these things. Before you go any further, you need to discuss with your partner where those bonds or connections are weakest so you can connect with each other on firmer ground.

Connecting on an Emotional Level

It is very noticeable when couples are connected to each other emotionally. This may take some time, as not everyone likes expressing themselves emotionally. This can make it appear that you are not compatible, but this is not always the case. Some individuals need to feel very secure in a relationship before they can open up about their innermost feelings of fear, vulnerability, guilt, and low self-esteem.

When a relationship is more mature, those connections may have been made early on, but as time has passed, these links or bonds may have weakened in places, and the relationship has settled into a more superficial space.

If your relationship is settled, perhaps you now

need to think about those feelings of Europhobia when you fell in love - deliciously painful experience. All your senses are heightened, and you feel an overpowering sense of joy. Usually, it takes a little time for strong bonds to grow out of this "falling in love" period. Your feelings are too intense to notice that perhaps your partner does not feel the same way as you do about this affair. But if love is real, you will connect to your partner in ways that convince you that you want to spend the rest of your life with them.

If these feelings are not returned after a time, then you could be moving into an unhealthy relationship in which you give your all but get nothing in return. This is why you have important conversations before you commit to a long-term relationship and why have meaningful conversations with your partner if you wish to rekindle the love you felt for each other all those years ago.

Friends for Life

Being friends is an important part of rekindling the spark in a relationship. After all, you started off as friends. You need to find the root of this friendship to ensure it hasn't died through lack of sustenance. Often couples drift apart because they no longer see each other as friends, but rather, as fellow travelers on the journey of life – albeit travelers with a common destination. To connect socially and emotionally, share hobbies and activities.

This way, you are engaging as a couple rather than

two individuals. That does not mean you have to lose your own independence – far from it. By being independent individuals, you are more likely to want to share hobbies too. Ask yourself how much time per week you spend on mutual hobbies and interests. It's likely you did so in the beginning of your love journey; if you want to rekindle the spark, it's time to link up again and build some worthwhile social connections.

Tips for Having a Fulfilling Relationship

Start Here

Connect to the one you love. Share your innermost thoughts and feelings with the person you love and trust.

Remember the feelings of joy and happiness you felt when you first met. Meditate on those feelings and manifest them in your everyday life.

Be connected to yourself. Dig deep into your soul and unearth those feelings of negativity that creep into your daily activities. Are you clingy, are you dominating? What forces are keeping you from connecting to your partner?

Don't be unrealistic. It's fine to be a dreamer, many people are, but life is not a romantic novel or a movie that all ends up absolutely perfect. Life is challenging, and relationships are challenging. Travel together hand in hand, and you may find life is beautiful most of the time.

Learn from one another. Look closely at your

partner, what do you see. What is being reflected back at you? Learn to grow together, learn to be better people together, and share the joys, trials, and tribulations that make up this rich tapestry called life.

Enjoy the Beauty That a Relationship Brings

Imagine the perfect relationship. What do you see? You probably will see things you don't see in your own relationship. This is because you are too close. Your relationship is beautiful, but you have become blinded by the petty problems and hard realities of life. So, let's take a little journey to this beautiful land that is your relationship.

The beauty of a good relationship is that you feel comfortable in your own skin. There are no critics in your relationship, only loving-kindness. You are just as happy alone as you are with your partner. Enjoy this security; you have earned it. Enjoy that you don't let the sun go down on your disagreements. A beautiful relationship is one where arguments and petty fights are nipped in the bud. Don't use silly arguments as a reason to test your partner, or to play silly "let's make up" games. Instead, discuss issues before they turn into conflict.

Enjoy your beautiful relationship by being grateful and enjoying what you have both achieved in your relationship as individuals and as a loving couple. Feel blessed, and don't put unrealistic barriers in your path. Aim for the heights while recognizing that life doesn't always give you what you want; it's no fairytale, it's you being the best person you can be. People in beautiful relationships see ordinary things in their lives as joyous. You and your partner cuddle up on the sofa watching a sad movie and laughing as you pass each other the tissues; that's the real fairytale.

Enjoy your beautiful relationship. Know that all relationships, brand new or seasoned, have their up and downs. This is normal, and you should not expect to be constantly happy. Happiness is fleeting, while contentment lasts longer. Be content. Be prepared to take that rollercoaster; hold on tight and enjoy the ride. Life is beautiful.

Enjoy the sense of freedom and individuality you have in your relationship. Recognize that you are both secure and protected from accusations and recriminations. Think only the best of your partner and you will receive the best. Grow together as people. Grow together knowing that your relationship may comprise ordinary ingredients such as respect, love, honor, and loyalty, but blended, they make a lovely relationship.

KEY TAKEAWAYS

- Remember how you felt when you first met your partner. Bring back these feelings of joy and romance. Take a beautiful walk in the moonlight, hold hands at the movies.

- Cultivate new hobbies together. Be a little bit daring; try something that pushes you out of your comfort zone.

- Get used to touching each other again. Feel how good your hand feels wrapped in his or her hand. Feel the warmth of skin-on-skin, just standing close together.

- Be crazy; do crazy things together. Find the inner child inside yourselves. Have some fun.

- It's always good to talk. Don't hide your feelings. Talk to your partner and, more important, listen to what they have to say, too.

- Connect with your partner emotionally and spiritually.

- Be friends. You become friends when you met, rekindle that friendship as you journey through life together.

- Be grateful for your beautiful relationship. Be realistic and be yourself.

- Your relationship is beautiful.

Rekindling and maintaining a beautiful relationship is hard work. It requires soul searching and honesty in your approach to yourself and your partner. In doing this, you must be kind to yourself. The following chapter shows you how self-help through meditation, mindfulness, and exercise can help you detox your mind so you can ease your relationship anxiety and build a lovely and lasting relationship.

Don't Forget to Claim:
YOUR FREE BONUS - 30-Days of Relationship Affirmations eBook!

As a way of thanking you for your purchase, I have a **free bonus** to offer you.

In addition to the information already provided in this book, I have created the *30-Days of Relationship Affirmations* eBook which provides you with 30 ready-made daily relationship affirmations. These will help you overcome any relationship roadblocks and strengthen your mind so that you can enjoy a more loving and intimate relationship.

Click (or tap) below to get your FREE Bonus instantly.

Click here:
www.mangobroom.com/relationship-affirmations/

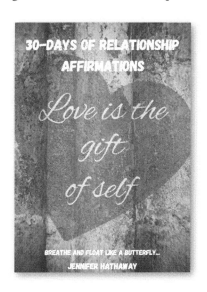

CHAPTER NINE
Detox Your Mind

(I BEGAN MEDITATING AFTER the breakdown of my relationship. I was devastated, and I just couldn't stop the chatter in my head. I kept running through the same questions over and over in my head. Not a moment went by that I wasn't trying to change the story in my head. Why did he do that to me? Could I have done things differently? One thing I knew for sure was that I was broken, and if I wanted to mend and carry on with my life, I had to find a way out of the toxic maze I was living in. A friend introduced me to meditation and mindfulness, and I have cleaned out the negativity in my head and am now able to offer someone the very best of me." (Shirley, age 37)

Meditation was once thought to be something mystical and unattainable to ordinary people. You had to go to India and sit with a yogi to learn how to speak to the universe. Or, at least that's what people thought. Now, meditation has gained a lot of ground, and people all over the world are learning how to use meditation every day to ease anxiety and live more fulfilled lives. These sections will guide you through some principles involved in meditation, mindfulness, and exercise to ease relationship anxiety and bring contentedness to turbulent lives.

Why Meditate?

If you think that meditation takes up lots of time and you must sit in awkward positions while humming, think again. Meditation is a wonderful aid to health and well-being and can take as little as 10 to 20 minutes each day. Many studies have been conducted on the benefits of practicing meditation; medical experts believe that just 20 minutes of meditation a day can lower blood pressure, decrease stress, and boost the immune system. It is recommended for heart health and improves mental health. With all these benefits, not surprisingly, it is now recommended for all levels of stress and anxiety and is becoming one of the leading aids in self-help and self-improvement. (Selig, 2017)

Meditating every day is something that must be learned. Some say that the mind requires at least 21 days for new habits to take root, the reason so many self-help videos and audiotapes suggest listening for 21 days. Meditation and positive thought practices do not require long periods; just a few minutes after you rise in the morning or to refresh your energy mid-afternoon is all that it takes to calm anxieties and relieve stress. Short bursts of meditation are proving to be greatly beneficial and can be done while sitting at your desk at work or in the park at lunchtime. Some especially useful meditation practices can be done in as little as five minutes, so there is really no excuse not to include meditation in your daily self-help routine.

Meditation Techniques

To become adept at meditating does take a little time when you first start. You need to acknowledge that your mind is full of chatter; it is noisy and disruptive, and the conversations you conduct in your head are numerous and often argumentative.

Begin by finding a comfortable place to sit or lie down. You can sit in the traditional yoga position if you if you find it agreeable (Being comfortable is the very important!) You don't want to be distracted because your legs have gone to sleep or your back hurts.

Once you are settled in, gently close your eyes. Take a deep breath and hold for four seconds, and release slowly for four seconds; repeat this three times. Now conduct a body scan. Just let your senses scan over your body. Do you recognize areas of stress? Tension can usually be found in the head and neck. Just relax your muscles. Let go of any tension. With practice, you can do this any time of the day and alongside anything you might be doing. Learn to relax the tense muscles.

Next, you need to concentrate only on your breath. This technique was discussed earlier in the book and is practiced in meditation and mindfulness. Focus on deep breathing, as this automatically relaxes the body.

As you focus only on your breathing, you may notice that your mind wanders. Pull it back to the present. In the present moment, all you are doing is breathing; nothing more, nothing less.

Now is the time to think only positive thoughts. "I am calm. I am content, I am happy, I am grateful." Each time your mind travels back to the past or into the future, pull it back to the present. This calms stress and lowers the heart rate. You may find it difficult to keep your mind in the present and may only do so for short bursts of time before the chatter returns in your head. But be positive and know that with practice, you can shut down the turbulence in your head and replace it with calm. Practice at least once a day for around 10 minutes if you have the time, but it is just as useful to break up the time and meditate for three or four minutes at a time. The idea is to empty your mind and enter the present. The present is your breath.

Practice Mindfulness

Mindfulness works on the same principle as meditation. It aids concentration, and it dramatically eases anxiety. Mindfulness can be termed as paying attention: concentrating on what is going on around you in relation to what you are seeing, hearing, smelling, and touching. For a few minutes every day, practice mindfulness. You can do it anywhere in any place. For the purpose of this example, imagine you are walking down the street in your hometown. It is a street you are familiar with. You know every crack in the sidewalk. But today you will take this walk mindfully.

As you walk along, think about what you can hear. Listen carefully. Are there birds singing? Can you hear the hum of traffic or children laughing? What can you smell? Is it gas fumes or is it the scent of flowers coming from a nearby window box? Watch the people walking past. Smile and acknowledge them. You will notice for that short walk along the street your mind has been entirely in the present. The worries and noise in your mind when you began your walk faded away, just for a short while. Health experts believe that mindfulness practiced just a few times in the day can reduce anxiety and stress levels significantly and is the equivalent of taking a short vacation in terms of reducing tensions in the body.

Being mindful means exactly that. You are focusing on the present. There is no past and no future, only now.

Mindfulness is one of the fastest growing stress-lowering techniques used today. Becoming proficient in mindfulness helps you to focus on your work. It teaches you how to concentrate and remain focused. In practical terms, it makes you a better listener and a better observer.

Mindful listening brings enormous rewards because you notice the nuances in people's words and how their body language might say something different from the words leaving their mouths. In relationships, mindful listening contributes to a better understanding of your partner's needs. You become more empathic and attentive. You will soon become recognized as someone caring and considerate.

Do Not Forget to Exercise

Along with calming your mind, you must also calm your body. So, *exercise*. Regular exercise makes you feel happier and more in control. It also helps you live longer and helps fight illness. It has now become an impossibility to ignore the benefits of exercise. Whether you are young or elderly, exercise improves your health and well-being. Exercise helps you maintain good body weight, and if you do aerobic exercise, you can burn off calories that could quickly turn to fat in your body.

Medical research now shows that regular exercise, taken at least three to four times a week, can fight illness and protect against heart disease. By being active every day, cholesterol levels are lowered, and the risk of type 2 diabetes and heart attacks are significantly lowered. It is now common to see educational literature in hospitals and doctors' offices showing how exercise can reduce the chances of type 2 diabetes, anxiety, and depression. Exercise also reduces the chances of some types of cancer, high blood pressure, and strokes. Medical doctors also recommend regular exercise to control arthritis and to prevent falls in later life.

If you are experiencing relationship anxiety or anxiety in general, exercise can provide you with an emotional lift. If you have had a stressful day or a fight with a loved one, taking a brisk walk will calm your nerves and boost your energy. You will also find you will sleep better when exercising regularly. You can fall asleep easier without the usual tossing and turning. However, exercising late at night is not recommended because you will become energized and not be able to settle enough to sleep. The harder you exercise, the more stamina you will have and thus more energy to cope with the daily stresses of work and home. Always check with your doctor before embarking on vigorous exercise regimes.

Simple Home Exercises

If you haven't exercised for a while, you need to start slowly. Don't rush into tough exercise regimes that could hurt you because you are then defeating the purpose of getting fit. A popular and inexpensive way to start home exercises is simple yoga stretches. Spend around 10 minutes a day stretching, and within a matter of weeks, you will be amazed at how different you feel physically and mentally.

An effective exercise to gently tone the core is lying on your right side, on a yoga mat, with your head propped up on your arm. Now gently lift your left leg as far as it will go without it hurting. It doesn't matter how far you can lift it, as you will get better as your muscles become supple. Hold the position for a count of five and lower. Repeat this three times and then change your position to the left side. When the exercise is completed, lie on your back and repeat the exercise.

Sit-ups and press-ups are also good home exercises

– as is jogging in place. A popular exercise for inside or out is jumping rope. This keeps you fit and is good aerobic exercise. Simple squats help to make limbs supply and are good for the circulation. Make sure when exercising at home you have a clear space to exercise. It is unnecessary to have a strict regime or to buy expensive equipment.

There are many YouTube videos available to show you how to exercise with minimum risk. Another exercise that many people overlook when preparing a home exercise regime is dancing. A 20-minute dance session can be the equivalent of walking one mile. Dance, smile, and be happy. Nothing lifts depression quicker or eases anxiety better. Turn the radio on and dance. If you have someone to dance with, all the better!

Simple Gym Exercises

Joining a gym can be daunting, especially when you see the myriad of equipment available. Usually, a trainer will introduce you to different equipment and show you how to use it. Walking and bicycle machines are the best equipment to use. Start off slowly and increase your speeds as your muscles get stronger. The walking machine speed can be adjusted to increase your walk to a jog, and then to a run. A 45-minute to an hour workout is a good, but remember to drink plenty of water and check with your doctor if you have any underlying health conditions.

There is no need to buy expensive gym wear; leggings or shorts are comfortable, along with a baggy tee shirt. Good sneakers are useful if you intend to use the treadmill. Floor exercises are good for beginners. Try holding a small dumbbell in each hand, then lunge forward on your left leg. Hold it for around three seconds and push back off and return to your start position. Once you get used to the gym and the equipment, you will benefit from a wide range of exercises, and improve your mental health and well-being.

KEY TAKEAWAYS

- Meditation significantly reduces blood pressure, stress levels, and anxiety
- The practice of mindfulness aids concentration, and mental awareness
- Exercise contributes to heart health, mental health and helps combat certain types of cancer and type 2 diabetes.
- Home exercise can be practiced at any time and costs nothing.
- Simple gym exercises can help with weight loss, body toning and reduces stress and anxiety.

Detoxing your mind and regular exercise helps reduce relationship anxiety and anxiety in general. You will feel better and to look better. With less stress in your life, you can enjoy your new relationships, but to love your partner, you need to love yourself first. The final chapter offers you a 7-day self-love challenge to take you forward into your next romantic adventure.

CHAPTER TEN
7-Day Self-love Challenge

((*'LL BE HONEST. My default setting toward myself is, at best, tolerance, and, at worst, merciless judgment. Left unchecked, I talk to myself with a toxic combination of scolding-mother and disdainful-teen. (Why am I so stinkin' sensitive? Why did I say that dumb thing? How could I possibly lose my cell phone in the house again? Why can't I keep the bathroom floor clean? Sheesh, my hair is ridiculous.)*

These voices are so natural and familiar to me that, for a long while, I didn't realize they existed. But one day, my therapist asked if I would speak to another person the way I talk to myself, and I was mortified: Are you kidding?! Never…

I began to wonder what might happen if I changed that voice".

(Julie Rybarczyk: 2018, cited in https://witanddelight.com/2018/03/how-i-learned-to-love-myself/)

These words tell of a personal journey of self-discovery and a quest to learning how to love oneself. This final chapter allows you to take the 7-day challenge in your own personal quest to love yourself and discover a healthier and happier you.

Self-Love

Medical experts believe that self-love is a key ingredient in happiness and well-being. RuPaul said, *"If you can't love yourself, how in the hell, are you gonna love somebody else?"* This is a truism. If you don't love yourself, then you cannot love anyone else. Beauty is all around us, but it is also inside each of us, too. You must reach into your soul and recognize the beauty hidden within.

This is more important in the world today, as image becomes more important than substance and social media questions and probes your every move. When you learn to love yourself, you open the floodgates to the beauty within, and your self-expression emerges like a butterfly from the chrysalis of self-doubt you may have nurtured most of your life.

By learning to love yourself, you take control of your life, becoming empowered by decisions that are informed and calculated, achieving best results. Your physical and mental agility blossoms. Loving yourself will bolster your confidence and boost your ability to face life's adversities. You will become a better version of yourself, and life will take on a new meaning.

The 7-Day Self-Love Challenge That Helps You to be More Centered and Less Anxious

Day One: Meditation

It's time to detox your mind and begin to love yourself. You have within you the power to unlock your true
self. Center your being, focusing only on your breath.
Do this three times today. Pull your mind back to the
present each time it wanders. Make no judgments, just
return to your breath while you are mediating concentrate on the present moment. Leave the past where it
belongs: in the past. You cannot change the past. It has
been written; it cannot be changed. Leave it be; it's too
late for "if only." Don't dwell in the future.

The future has not been written yet. No one knows
what is in store. You cannot live in a future that does
not yet exist. Live in the moment. As long as you meditate, as long as you focus only on your breath, you will
live in the present. Your mind will be open to positive
thoughts. "I am healthy, wealthy, loved, and wise."

Day Two: Mindfulness

The benefits of practicing mindfulness are bounti-
ful. You will become more attentive, you will become
an active listener, and you will gain confidence and
self-esteem. Four or five times today, practice mindfulness. Pay attention to what is going on around
you. Notice how your senses come alive. Listen to the
sounds in your environment. This could be the soft

131

hum of the air conditioning or the clicking of heels on a tiled floor. You may smell the grass beneath your feet or notice how your hand feels on an escalator rail. Practicing mindfulness is shown to reduce blood pressure and ease anxiety significantly.

Day Three: Accept Who You Are

Self-acceptance can be a tricky challenge. At some point in their lives, people may find it difficult to accept who they are based on disappointments, unfulfilled expectations, and misjudgments. You are no different. How others perceive you can affect your perception of yourself more strongly than anything else that impacts your life. But if you don't see yourself for who you are, then you can't expect others to do the same. Accept who you are and love who you are. You are unique. You are beautiful, and you are you. By loving yourself, you are permitting yourself to be compassionate and kind to yourself. Your inner beauty will shine through, and your anxieties will disappear into the void.

Today find somewhere quiet to sit and just for a few minutes contemplating a particular challenge you are experiencing. See yourself dealing with challenges. Get centered. Ask yourself why this is a difficult challenge. Be kind to yourself. What is within your control, and what is not? Deal with what you can deal with and leave what is out of your control. You are not superhuman. You are just you. Carefully work out a plan to resolve your challenge. Be positive. See the challenge in your mind's eye. Work it out carefully and logically.

Day Four: Putting Yourself at the Head of the Line

This is another tricky challenge. You may have been taught from an early age that putting yourself first is not the expected thing for you to do. Changing your mindset on this aspect of self-love can be difficult, but necessary. Learn to put your emotions first before the emotions of others. This makes logical sense. If you don't practice this fundamental rule, then you will find yourself at the mercy of others. You will be tossed and blown on the whims of others. When you put others first before yourself, you are telling yourself you are not as worthy as they are. This is not true, and you've always known this. But old habits die hard.

Today is when you begin to put yourself first. Don't stand at the back of the line because there may not be anything left when you arrive at the table. Think about what you want to do with your life. List the things you crave. This is not a selfish wish list. This is you recognizing that you are deserving and worthy of putting yourself first. If you are a caring person, you will want to put the needs of others first, but if you don't sustain your love for yourself, then you will not have the inner strength to attend to the needs of others properly.

Day Five: Self-Care

Today is the day you set about mapping out your self-care regime. Self-care is about thinking about you and how you intend to sustain a healthy, wholesome lifestyle. For example, think about what you eat. Does

133

your diet need adjusting to suit you rather than suiting others?

This can be seen as being selfish, but you must begin thinking about it differently. What is healthy for you will be healthy for those you prepare meals for. It is time to unlock the real you and love the person you are. Consider other aspects of your life. Do you go to bed too late in the evening? Do you work long hours to please your boss? Do you do more than your fair share of household chores while others in the household excuse themselves? Learning self-care takes time and effort in your part, but you are more than worthy of the effort.

Day Six: Find Your Inner Child

When was the last time you had some fun? Health experts advise us to laugh out loud every day. When was the last time you laughed out loud? Or you were so caught up in laughter you could barely stand up? While no one can realistically hope to laugh hysterically all day and every day, notice how often you smile in a day.

Today's challenge requires that you smile all day. A tall order, yes, but feeling happy is something that you can choose to do from the moment you open your eyes in the morning. We have a choice. We can be gloomy or happy. Choose happily. Find that small child that lives inside you. Bring her into the light. That inner child is part of the unique you that requires your love and affection. Many people find their inner child with music and dance. Today find a few minutes to play some music, dance, and sing. Love who you are.

Day Seven: Thank You, Thank You, Thank You

Today be grateful for everything you have. When you forget to be grateful, you forget to be happy. Life becomes colorless: a drudge. When you look around at the cruelties of this world and the sorrow endured by some people as they journey through life, it can sometimes be difficult to be happy. But it is up to you to find the beauty in the world and be grateful for it.

Think about the best sunset you have ever seen or the most beautiful landscape. Remind yourself how it feels to hold a newborn baby and the joy you feel when you witness human acts of kindness. There is much to be grateful for. On this last day of your 7-day challenge, take some time to think about the beauty that surrounds and sustains you. Think about the beauty within yourself and say thank you, thank you, thank you.

KEY TAKEAWAYS

- It takes 21 days to change a habit. In just seven days, you can begin to change the habits of a lifetime. In three weeks, you can learn to love yourself.

- Put yourself first. Don't spend your entire life trying to make life better for others before you make it better for yourself.

- Living within you is a beautiful being. Learn to love that beautiful being. Learn to recognize the beauty that surrounds you and say thank you for the blessings in your life.

CONCLUSION

" I N THIS WORLD, *we all have a responsibility to treat people with respect. We live, love, and respect, while we are here on this Earth. How you view this world and the people around you depends on how much you are prepared to love yourself and to love those around you. Intimate relationships are the way people seek support, love, and attachment. Some individuals abuse those who join in union with them, disrespecting them, controlling them, and mocking them. Others find relationships stressful and difficult to maintain. What everyone seeks, in the end, is a beautiful relationship that provides sustenance and love.*" (Author)

This book guides readers through strategies and exercises to reduce relationship anxiety. It has sought to provide encouragement and advice on how to improve relationships and become better people. It culminates with a message of hope for those struggling with anxiety in their quest to discover a beautiful relationship.

Its overarching goal was to provide a simple, accessible guide to what relationship anxiety is and how to combat it. In doing so, it made a variety of observations and drew several conclusions.

Anxiety is a normal reaction to threat, especially when that threat comes between you and your partner. Anxiety becomes problematic when it causes emotional distress that damages our health and wellbeing. Relationship anxiety can turn to jealousy, anger, and even hate. Over-imagination and false perceptions are constant companions of those who experience anxiety in their relationships. When individuals feel threatened by the relationships they are caught up in, they will sabotage that relationship to avoid making a commitment.

Relationship anxiety often stems from feelings of insecurity and low self-esteem. These emotions can be traced back to childhood experiences of poor attachment, or they are fostered by bad experiences in previous relationships. Sometimes, individuals contribute to the anxieties of their partners by undermining their worth. However, for many individuals, the mere fact of being in a relationship brings about intense feelings of insecurity, and they often end up in failed relationships or are controlled by domineering partners. Self-silencing habits can result in the ill-health of the dominated partner.

Everyone tends to over-think. Over-thinking is common in people who experience relationship anxiety. Those who over-analyze every little thing, find relationships difficult to manage. This is because they expect their partners to fix their problems. They want their partners to show their love by making their insecurities go away. This can't be done. Often small irritants can turn into big issues that result in conflict and unhappiness, which further exasperates anxiety.

This book has offered a range of strategies and exercises to help readers to overcome relationship anxiety. There are many ways to manage anxiety and many strategies to achieve a calm, beautiful relationship so many searches for. Some deep-rooted issues can be addressed professionally by therapists, but for the most part, successful results can be achieved by practicing the suggestions within these pages.

To begin, relationship anxiety can be eased by recognizing that relationships can be ruined when control is used to manipulate partners. Anxiety can damage sex lives and inhibit demonstrations of loving intimacy. By learning to love your body, you can learn to love and trust your partner. When relationship anxiety plays a significant role in inhibiting your sex life, it is time to explore your own sexuality and the expectations of your partner. Don't turn a blind eye to the many studies that discuss anxiety in intimate relationships. Learn to recognize the anxiety issues you carry with you into each new relationship.

Being positive about yourself and not making comparisons with those around you reduces your level of stress and anxiety. Learn to talk to each other honestly about your fears. Effective and mindful conversations between partners enhance the ability to break down the barriers that contribute to relationship anxiety.

Nurture your freedoms and independence and respect your partner's independence too. Take the time to practice mindfulness and meditation. Be present in your relationship, learn to pay attention to what is going on around you, and attempt to live in the present as often as you can. Meditation and mindfulness help reduce anxiety and stress levels and contributes to good health and well-being.

Place your trust in your partner and be true to yourself. Learn to love yourself before you love others. Put yourself at the front of the line and recognize your own worth. Only in this way can you genuinely love others.

Relationship anxiety can be addressed, and it can be healed. Draw inspiration from the pages of this book. Return to any of the chapters when you feel the need for encouragement. Know that the underlying message in this book is that *you are not alone in your anxiety*. The personal stories heading each chapter are there to remind you of this. Stop living inside your head and recognize the power you hold within you.

Remember that each one of us is beautiful and unique. We need not live in the shadow of others. Every one of us seeks a loving and fulfilling relationship. To feel anxious is to be normal. We need to know the worth of people before we place our trust in them. As we learn to trust, we learn to manage our anxieties. A beautiful relationship is just around the corner if you pay attention and love yourself with the same passion you hope others will love you.

May I ask you a small favor?

If you enjoyed this book and got helpful pointers and actionable strategies from it, **would you consider letting others know about it?**

Here a several ways you can do so:

1. Leave a review on Amazon
2. Leave a review at Goodreads
3. Tell your peeps about it on your **Blog, Podcast** or **YouTube** Channel
4. Share it on **Facebook, Instagram, Twitter, Pinterest** or **LinkedIn**
5. Mention it to your **friends and family members** - or your colleagues at work

Reviews on Amazon are incredibly helpful - both for other readers to decide whether this book will be useful to them and for indie authors and publishers to get the word out about our books. Your support is much appreciated!

Thanks in advance for your good deeds!
You are a STAR...:)

Warm regards,
Jennifer Hathaway

Don't Forget to Claim:
YOUR FREE BONUS - 30-Days of Relationship Affirmations eBook!

As a way of thanking you for your purchase, I have a **free bonus** to offer you.

In addition to the information already provided in this book, I have created the *30-Days of Relationship Affirmations* eBook which provides you with 30 ready-made daily relationship affirmations. These will help you overcome any relationship roadblocks and strengthen your mind so that you can enjoy a more loving and intimate relationship.

Click (or tap) below to get your FREE Bonus instantly.

Click here:

www.mangobroom.com/relationship-affirmations/

REFERENCES

Ackerman, Courtney. 2020. "What is Attachment Theory? Bowlby's 4 stages Explained" https://positive-psychology.com/attachment-theory/

Balarezo, D., 2019. "Why we Sabotage Romantic Relationships – and What We Can Do About It." https://ideas.ted.com/why-we-sabotage-romantic-relationships-and-what-we-can-do-about-it/

Baum, I. 2016. "11 Ways to Know You're Ready to Start Dating Again, According to Experts" https://www.bustle.com/articles/166862-11-ways-to-know-youre-ready-to-start-dating-again-according-to-experts

Barron, A., 2020. "7 Tips for Dating If you Have Anxiety". https://www.boundless.org/blog/7-tips-for-dating-if-you-have-anxiety/

Bronner, S. J. 2020 "Mind and Body" https://www.inverse.com/article/59500-self-silencing-relationship-health

Chopra, N. 2020. "10 Tangible Thought-Provoking Ways to Practice Self-Love". https://www.

145

mindbodygreen.com/0-12428/10-wonderful-ways-to-practice-selflove.html

Clarke, A, H. 2019 "Why do Relationship Insecurities Generate So much Anxiety"? https://www.psychologytoday.com/gb/blog/hack-your-anxiety/201902/why-do-relationship-insecurities-generate-so-much-anxiety

Christensen, S. P., 2018. Social Media Use and its Impact on Relationships and Emotions, Provo. UT. Brigham Young University

Dixit, J., 2020. "How Small Irritants become BIG Relationship Issues…and what to do about it." https://throughyourbody.com/how-small-irritants-become-big-relationship-issuesand-what-you-can-do-about-it/

Eckel, S., 2016. "Listening to Jealousy." https://www.psychologytoday.com/gb/articles/201611/listening-jealousy

Good Therapy. 2020. "Commitment Issues." https://www.goodtherapy.org/learn-about-therapy/issues/commitment-issues

Hall, J., 2020. "Distancing Strategies, the Love Avoidant Uses to avoid Intimacy" https://www.loveaddictionhelp.com/12-distancing-strategies-the-love-avoidant-uses-to-avoid-intimacy

Healthline. 2020. "How to Handle Relationship Anxiety" https://www.healthline.com/health/relationship-anxiety

Jalili, C. 2019 "Feeling Lonely in your Relationship? Here's What to do About it" https://time.com/5548386/feeling-lonely-in-relationship/

Khoshaba, D., 2012. "A Seven-Day Prescription for Self-Love" https://www.psychologytoday.com/gb/blog/get-hardy/201203/seven-step-prescription-self-love

Lancer, D., 2018. "Dealing with a Passive-Aggressive Partner." https://psychcentral.com/lib/dealing-with-a-passive-aggressive-partner/

Mayer Robinson, K. 2020 "How to Rekindle the Spark in Your Relationship" https://www.webmd.com/sex-relationships/features/rekindle-romance#1

Mayo Clinic. 2020. "Exercise: 7 Benefits of Physical Activity". https://www.mayoclinic.org/healthy-lifestyle/fitness/in-depth/exercise/art-20048389#:~:text=Regular%20physical%20activity%20can%20improve,energy%20to%20tackle%20daily%20chores.

Medical News Today. 2020. "Why Self-help is important and how to cultivate it" https://www.medicalnewstoday.com/articles/321309#The-ills-of-perfectionism

Medical News Today. 2020. "What is Relationship Anxiety?" https://www.medicalnewstoday.com/articles/relationship-anxiety

Mindful. 2020. "Top Ten Reasons to Meditate" https://www.mindful.org/top-10-reasons-to-meditate/

Newman, L., 2020. "10 Ways to Create a Strong, Intimate Relationship". https://tinybuddha.com/blog/10-ways-to-create-a-strong-intimate-relationships/

Pumphrey, C., 2016. "Couples Who Are Truly in Love Connect in These 5 Ways". https://www.womenshealthmag.com/relationships/a19976554/ways-to-connect-with-partner/

Rybarczyk, J., 2018. "How I learned to love myself" https://witanddelight.com/2018/03/how-i-learned-to-love-myself/

Selig, M., 2017. "12 Quick Mini-Meditations to Calm Your Mind and Body". https://www.psychologytoday.com/gb/blog/changepower/201703/12-quick-mini-meditations-calm-your-mind-and-body

Seltzer, L F., 2016. "Self-Absorption: The Root of All (Psychological) Evil?" https://www.psychologytoday.com/gb/blog/evolution-the-self/201608/self-absorption-the-root-all-psychological-evil

Shondell. 2016. "Top 12 Worst Jealous Rages in Hollywood" https://www.therichest.com/entertainment/top-12-worst-jealous-rages-in-hollywood/

Smith, A., 2010. "Help, My Controlling Behavior is Ruining Relationships." https://www.psychology-today.com/gb/blog/healthy-connections/201007/help-my-controlling-behavior-is-ruining-relationships

Tsangarides, L., 2018. "Is Social media Damaging Your Relationship"? https://psychcentral.com/blog/is-social-media-damaging-your-romantic-relationship/

Tye, K. 2020. "How Anxiety Destroys Relationships (And How to Stop It)" https://thriveglobal.com/

stories/how-anxiety-destroys-relationships-and-how-to-stop-it/

Very Well Mind. 2020. "How Anxiety May Affect Your Relationship." https://www.verywellmind.com/how-anxiety-can-cause-relationship-prob-lems-1393090

Whitborne, S.K., 2012. "Why Clingy Partners Cling." https://www.psychologytoday.com/gb/blog/fulfillment-any-age/201209/why-clingy-partners-cling

Yacaub, C., Spoede, J., Cutting, R., Hawley, d. 2018. "The Impact of Social Media on Romantic Rela-tionships." https://zenodo.org/record/1490763#.Xtd33TpKjIU

Yearwood, D., 2020. "The Connection We Have." http://www.lovelifepoems.net/love-poem/you-are-the-one

Your Tango. 2020. "No Strings Attached" https://www.yourtango.com/2015254612/no-strings-at-tached-please-20-celebrity-commitment-phobes

Printed in Great Britain
by Amazon